Andrew Coltee Ducarel

A Repertory of the Endowments of Vicarages

In the Dioceses of Canterbury and Rochester

Andrew Coltee Ducarel

A Repertory of the Endowments of Vicarages
In the Dioceses of Canterbury and Rochester

ISBN/EAN: 9783337059224

Printed in Europe, USA, Canada, Australia, Japan

Cover: Foto ©ninafisch / pixelio.de

More available books at **www.hansebooks.com**

A REPERTORY

OF THE

ENDOWMENTS OF VICARAGES

In the DIOCESES of

CANTERBURY and ROCHESTER,

By Dr. DUCAREL, F. R. and A. SS.

COMMISSARY of the CITY and DIOCESE of
CANTERBURY.

LONDON,
PRINTED BY J. NICHOLS.
M.DCC.LXXXII.

[Price 3s. 6d.]

ADVERTISEMENT.

THIS Repertory of the Endowments of Vicarages in the Diocese of Canterbury, is a Second Edition of a Work printed in 4to in 1763. It is now much enlarged and improved by many Discoveries made since that Time in the Records, Registers, &c. of the See of Canterbury, and those of the Dean and Chapter of that Cathedral.

To this Edition the Author has added the best Account he hath been able to collect of the Endowments of

[iv]

Vicarages in the Diocese of Rochester; which (imperfect as it is) will, He hopes, prove acceptable to the Gentlemen and Clergy of the County of Kent.

Doctors Commons,
Oct. 7, 1781.

[1]

A REPERTORY

OF THE

ENDOWMENTS of VICARAGES

IN THE

DIOCESE of CANTERBURY.

ALDINGTON, Capella. See THOR-NEHAM, Vic.

ALDINTONE, Rect. olim. Vic. hodie Allington cum Capella de Smeeth. Ordinatio Vicariæ. Dat. 3. Non. Feb. A. D. 1295. Reg. Winchelsea, fol. 195. a. (MSS. Lambeth.) Concerning the Tithes and a Modus in this parish, see the Case of Chapman v. Smith (July 17, 1754). In Vezey's Reports, vol. II. p. 506.

ALKHAM,

DIOCESE OF

ALKHAM, Vic.

A Terrier of all the Glebe Lands, Meadows, Gardens, Orchards, Houses, and Portions of Tithes, belonging both to the Parsonage and Vicarage of the Parish of Alkham, taken by the Minister and sworn officers, at the Metropolitical Visitation of Archbishop Laud, May 6, 1634.—Reg. Laud. Pars $1^{ma.}$ fol. 207. a. (MSS. Lambeth.)

APPLEDORE, olim APOLDRE. See COLREDE.

ASH cum Capell. de FLETE, olim Vic. hodie Cur. See NONNINGTON.

Vide Ordinationes et Statuta Eccl. Collegiat. de Wengham in Com. Cantii Regist. Peckham, fol. 32. a. (Printed in Monast. Ang. Tom. III. P. 2. fol. 52. et seq.)

Augmented by Archbishop Juxon 33l. 6s. 8d. per Ann. besides the old

old Penſion of 16l. 13s. 4d. By Indentures, one dated 20 Dec. 12, Car. II. another dated 10 Dec. 25 Car. II. Farther augmented 20l. by Indenture 17 April, 28 Car. II. (Lambeth Leaſes.)

ASHFORD, Vic.

Great ſpoil was made of the Vicar's Eſtates at the Reformation. Ponet was then Vicar, and Sir John Cheek the Receiver of ſuch ſpoil; both great Reformers. See Regiſt. of Chriſt Church, Canterbury (MS. of the late Rev. John Lewis, Miniſter of Mergate, p. 20. in the MS. Library at Lambeth, marked N° 1125 *.)

BAKECHILD, al. BAPCHILD, Vic.

Ordinatio Vicariæ per Dom. Ricardum (Whetherſhed) Cant. Archiep. Dat. et Act. Anno Incarnationis Domini 1229, Menſe Janu-

* Which will hereafter be called MS. Lewis.

arii.

arii.—Regift. Iflip. fol. 73. b. (MSS. Lambeth.)

Augmentatio Porcionis Vicarii Ecclefiæ Parochial. de Bacchild Cant. Diœc. Dat. 8 Novemb. 1435.— Regift. Chicheley pars $2^{da.}$ fol. 289. a. (MSS. Lambeth.)

Mandatum Prioris & Capituli Cant. Decano de Sydingbourne directum pro folutione Penfionis annue 40 Solid. Sterling. debit. a Decano & Capit. Ecclefiæ Ciceftren. Vicario Eccl. de Bakechild ex ordinatione antiqua Vicariæ dicte Ecclefiæ. Dat. Non. Januar. A. D. 1348.—Regift. P. par. 2. fol. 55. b. (MSS Cantuar.)

BEAKISBOURN, olim LIVINGEBURN, Vic.

Archbifhop Parker obtained an Augmentation to this Vicarage of 10l. four Quarters of Wheat, and eighteen Quarters of Barley, per Annum.

CANTERBURY.

Annum. —Harris's Hist. of Kent, p. 36.
Eadmundi Cant. Archiepi Confirmatio Eccl. de Livingeburn cum omnibus ad eam pertinent. Prior. et Convent. S^{ti}. Gregorii Cant. in proprios usus convertend. Salva vicaria decem marcarum ad presentat. dict. Prior. et Convent. et de horreis ad dict. Eccl. spectant in proprios usus convertend. Chartæ et concessiones factæ Canonicis S^{ti}. Gregorii Cantuar. fol. 66. MS. in the publick Library at Cambridge, marked Ll. 11. 15. Metæ et Bundæ paroch. de Beakisborn, 3 die Junii, anno 11 H. VI. In the Leiger Book of the Priory of St. Gregory, near Canterbury, fol. 128. a Copy whereof may be seen in MS. A. 11. fol. 93. a. in the Archives of Canterbury Cathedral. This Vicarage was augmented

mented by Abp. Juxon. Farther augmented by Indenture, dat. 17 April, 28 Car. II. ten Pounds. (L. L.*)

BEAUXFIELD, al. WHITFIELD, Vic.

Augmented by Archbishop Juxon 20l. per Annum; by Indenture, dat. Mar. 11$^{th.}$ 14 Car. II. and one dat. 4 Feb. 25 Car. II. (L. L.)
Compositio facta per Dom. Henricum (Chicheley) Cant. Arch. inter Prior. et Convent. de Cumbwell impropriatores Eccl. Paroch. de Beausfield, et Dom. Will. Geddyng, Vicar. perpet. Eccl. prædict. occasione Porcionis Vicariæ prædict. ac percepcionis Decimar. ac pensionum eidem Eccl. pertinent. Dat. London. 24 Die Maii. A. D. 1441. Regist. Chicheley, pars 1$^{ma.}$ fol. 236. a, b. (MSS. Lambeth.)

A Deed of Hen. Hamington, Vicar of Beausfield, alias Whitfield, where-

* i. e. Lambeth Leases.

by

by he renounces all the Right, Title, and Intereſt, that he had by virtue of a certain Compoſition made in the Time of Henry Chicheley, Abp. of Canterbury, between the then Vicar of Beausfield and the then Prior and Convent of Cumberwell. Dated June 26, 1613.—Reg. Abbott. Pars 1ma. fol. 397, a. b. (MS. Lambeth.)

BERFRESTONE, Rect.

This little Rectory, in the Patronage of St. John's College, Oxford, is now augmented by Queen Anne's Bounty, and 200l. raiſed by the ſaid College.

BETHERSDEN, Vic.

Abp. Juxon augmented this Vicarage out of the Great Tithes, 10l. per Ann. by Indenture, dated 17 April, 28 Car. II. (L. L.)

BIDDENDEN. Rect. See CRANEBROKE.

BOCLAND, alias BUCLAND, hodie Cur. Defcriptio limitum et finium paroch. de Bocland, Leiger Book of St. Martin at Dover, fol. 254, b. (MSS. Lambeth. N° 241.)
Augmented by Abp. Juxon. 12l. per Ann. By Indentures, dated 4 July, 13 Car. II. and another dated 10 March, 23 Car. II. (L. L.) Appropriatio dict. Eccl. Priorat. S^{ti}. Martini de Dover. Dat. apud Cherring, 8 Kal. Nov. A. D. 1364. Leiger Book of St. Martin Dover, fol. 107. a. (MSS. Lambeth.)

BOCTON fubtus le Blen, Vic.
Sententia Judicum delegat in caufa Decimar. provenient. de quodam fundo vulg. dict. Clyvemarfh infra parochiam de Bolton Underblane, inter Decan. et Capit. Cant. et alios partem appellant. et Robertum
Thomp-

CANTERBURY.

Thompson, Vicar de Bolton Underblane partem appellat. Dat. 20 Febr. A. D. 1567. (Chart. Antiq. R. 262. Archiv. Cantuar.)

BONINGTON, Rect.
Unio Ecclesiarum de Hurst al. Fawkenhurst et de Bonington. Dat. 16 die Nov. A. D. 1583. Reg. Whitgift, vol. I. fol. 449 (MSS. Lambeth.)

BOUGHTON, al. BOCTON ALUPHE, Vic. See WESTWELL.

BOXLE. Vic. See STURMOUTH.
Ordinatio Vicariæ. Dat. Id. Feb. A. D. 1377.—Reg. Sudbury, fol. 124. a, b. (MSS. Lambeth.) Several Instruments relating to this Church are printed from the Archives of the See of Rochester, in Dr. Thorpe's Regiftrum Roffenfe, p. 177 to p. 185.

Sententia super Decimis, dict. Vicarie A. D. 1403. Among the Chartæ Antiquæ

tiquæ in the Augmentation Office, marked D. 101. The vicar of Boxley has a Penſion of 8l. per Annum out of the Exchequer.

BRABOURNE, al. BRADBORNE, Vic. Augmented by Archbiſhop Juxon 16l. per Ann. By Indenture, dated 5 Sept. 13 Car. II. and another, dated 6 Oct. 23 Car. II. (L L.) Perambulation of the Pariſh of Brabourn, anno 10 Ric. I. and a copy of the Ordination of this Vicarage, is extant in a manuſcript marked A. 11. fol. 68. a. in the Archives of Canterbury Cathedral. Portio Vicar de Bradburne aſſignata d'no Thome de Banſtede, Vicar. Ibid. per Fratrem Hugonem de Faloniis, Priorem de Horton, A. D. 1445. Certificatio finium et limitacionum parochie de Braborne, anno 10 R. I. (i. e.) A. D. 1198.

1198. Regiſtr. Priorat. de Horton, Chart. 239. 241. 242. MS. penes Tho. Aſtle, Arm. 1781.

Bradsole. See Leysdown.

Bredgar, Vic.

Dotatio Vicariæ, dat. 8 die Nov. A. D. 1391. Reg. Morton. Dene Bourchier et Courtney, fol. 214. a. b. (MSS. Lambeth.)

Brokland, Vic. See Colrede.

Ordinatio Vicariæ. Dat. apud Otteford 15 Kal. Auguſt. A. D. 1360.— Regiſt. Iſlip. fol. 162. a. (MSS. Lambeth.) Printed in X. Scriptores col. 2087.

Ordinatio Vicariæ per Simonem Cant. Archiep. (Sans Date.) Regiſter of St. Auſtin, Cant. called the Blacke Boke, MS. in the Cotton Library (now in the Britiſh Muſeum) marked Fauſtina A. 1. fol. 232. b.

Bromfield. See Leeds.

Brook,

Brook, Rect.

Conventio inter Dominum Henricum Prior. et Convent. Eccl. Christi Cant. et Dominum Adam Rect. Eccl. B. M. de Broke, super Decimis, A. D. 1316. Chartular Eccl. Christi Cant. Chart. 135. et 136.

Cantuar. Civitas.

Unio Ecclesiarum S^{tæ}. Mildredæ, Omnium Sanctorum, ac S^{tæ}. Mariæ ad Castrum in civitat. Cantuar. Dat. apud Lambeth 29 die Septembr. 1684.—Licentia regia super unione predict. T. R. apud Westminster, 14 die Octob. A. D. 1684.—Reg. Sancroft fol. 252. a, b. (MSS. Lambeth.)

——————— S^{tæ}. Crucis Westgate, Vic.

Ordinatio Vicariæ S^{tæ}. Crucis Westgate, Cant. Dat. apud Saltwood, 5 Id. Junii, A. D. 1347.—(Printed in Somner's Antiq. of Canterbury, pag. 74 and 78.)

Copia

CANTERBURY. 13

Cantuar. Civitas.

Copia Compofitionis dict. vicariæ extat in MS. notat. A. 11. fol. 38. b. in Archiv. Eccl. Cathedral. Cantuarienfis.

Inquifitio ad quod dampnum fi dominus Rex concedat Simoni Tanner et aliis quod ipfi unum Mefuag. et unum Gardinum cum pertin. in parochia S^{tæ}. Crucis de Weftgate, Cantuar. dare poffint et affignare Roberto Raynhull, Vicar Ecclefiæ S^{tæ}. Crucis in Weftgate, et Succefforibus fuis, Capt. apud Cant. die Mercur. prox. ante feftum Nat. Beate Mar. Virg. Anno regnor Ric. Regis Angl. et Franciæ 16°. (Chartæ antiquæ A. 219.) Archiv. Cantuar.

―――――― S$^{ti.}$ Dunstani, Vic.

Ordinatio Vicariæ S^{ti} Dunftani, Cant. Dat. apud Mortlake 16 Kal. Aug.

Cantuar. Civitas.

Aug. A. D. 1322.—Regift. Reynolds, fol. 102. a. (MSS. Lambeth.) Printed in Somner's Antiquities of Canterbury, Appendix N° LXX. a. p. 74.

Augmentatio Vicariæ facta per Johem (Stratford) Cant. Archiepum, 3 Kal. Aug. A. D. 1342.—Statuens ut Conventus S^{ri}. Gregorii Cant. cui Ecclefia appropriata fuit, decimas minores, oblationes, &c. vicario olim affignate, annuam 2 marcarum penfionem perfolvat. (Liber de Rebus ad Archidiaconatum Cantuar. fpectantibus, Liber niger dictus in 8vo. fol. 42. — (MS. Wharton, p. 97. N° 582. MSS. Lambeth.)

In 1661 this vicarage was augmented out of the Great Tithes by Abp. Juxon. This Vicarage had 200l. given by Abp. Tenifon, by

CANTERBURY.

CANTUAR. Civitas.

which it enjoys Queen Anne's Bounty.

St. GREGORY's Priory, near Canterbury.

To this Priory of Regular Black Canons were appropriated the following Parfonages; viz. Betrichedene, St. Dunftan, Elmefted, Livingfborne, Natindon, North-Gate, Stallesford, Taninton, Waltham, and Weftgate. To the augmenting thefe Vicarages and Curacies, Abp. Juxon gave 210l. per Ann. out of the Great Tithes, A. D. 1661. Some of them were augmented 20l. per Annum, as Waltham and others. I fuppofe more or lefs, as the Abp. thought was needful. Bifhop Kennet (Cafe of Impropriations, p. 256.) fays, there were 2 or 13 Vicarages or Curacies belonging to this Priory.

But

DIOCESE OF

Cantuar. Civitas.

But I have hitherto met with no more than thefe ten.

————S^{tæ}. Margaretæ Eccl. Compofitio inter Rect. Eccl. S$^t_æ$. Margaretæ Cantuar. et Capellanos de Hofpitali pauperum Sacerdotum in Cantuaria, fuper oblationibus, obventionibus, &c. (fans Date.) Red Book of Canterbury, MS. in the Cotton Library (now in the Britifh Mufeum) marked Claudius D. X. fol. 100. b. 101. a.

————S^{ti}. Martini, Rect. Exemplification of a Decree of the Court of Firft-fruits, for reducing the Taxation of the Parfonage of Saint Marten withowte the Walles of Canterbury, from nyne Powndes per an. (at which Rate it was formerly charged with the Payment of Firft-fruits and Tenths) to 6l. 5s.

Cantuar. Civitas.

5s. 8d. Dat. 26 Nov. anno regni Reg. Edw^{di}. 6^{ti}. 1mo.
In which Decree is contained a Particular of the Tithes, &c. due to the Rector of the said Church. (Archiv. Cantuar.)

──────S^{tæ}. Mariæ Northgate,. Vic. Ordinatio Vicar. S. Mariæ Northgate Cantuar.—Jura Vicariæ—Hospitale de Northgate exceptum— Onera Vicarii (printed in Somner's Antiquity of Cant. Appendix, p. 73.) Declaratio per Robertum, Prior. ecclesiæ Christi Cant. et ejusdem loci Capitulum, sede Cant. vacante, Dat. 10 Kal. Novemb. A. D. 1348. super Ordinatione Vicariæ Beatæ Mariæ de Northgate Cant. que ordinata fuit, A. D. 1346. mensis Novemb. die 4°. (Registr. E. fol. 12.a.) MSS. Cantuar. Executio super Ordinatione Vicariæ

Cantuar. Civitas.

de Northgate, Dat. Cantuar. 10 Kal. Novemb. A. D. 1348. (Regift. P. fol. 54. b.) Ibid.

————— Eccl. B. M. de BREDENE et Sᴛɪ. EDMUNDI DE REDYNGATE. Unio dict. Ecclefiar. facta fede Cant. vacante per Prior. et Capit. Cant. 3 die Nov. A. D. 1349. (Reg. E. Eccl. Chrifti Cant.) fol. 46. a. b.

Eccl. B. M. ad CASTRUM et Sancti
————— JOHANNIS dicti Pauperis. Inquifitio fuper unione dict. Ecclefiar. 5 Kal. Julii, A. D. 1349. (Reg. Eccl. Chrifti Cant. fol. 46. b.)

————— Sti. PAULI. Vic. Ordinatio Vicar. Sti. Pauli Cantuar. —Refervata Rectori — Onera Vicarii—Jura Vicarii—Dat. 5 Id. Decemb. A. D. 1268. (printed in Somner's Antiquity of Cant. Appendix, pag.

pag. 73. and in X. Scriptores Col. 2095.)

A. D. 1268, a Vicarage was conſtituted here by Hugh Mortimer, Official to Boniface Archbiſhop of Canterbury, by the conſent of the Abbot of St. Auſtin, and Hamo Doge, Parſon of this Church, the laſt Rector here. The Vicar had all Obventions, Profits, &c. and was to pay the Archdeacon's Procurations, and all other uſual Onera. Dr. Harris's Hiſt. of Kent, p. 234.

———— S^{ti}. Petri, Rect.

Licentia Regis Edw^{di} 3$_{ti}$. conceſſa Richardo de Langedon, quod ipſe unum meſſuagium cum pertin. ſuis dare poſſit Thomæ Perſonæ S^{ti}. Petri Cant. pro manſo ſuo habend. ſibi et ſucceſſoribus ſuis Statuto de terris, &c. in manum mortuam non ponendis non obſtante. Dat. apud Weſtm.

Cantuar. Civitas.

Westm. 5 die Decemb. anno regni sui Angl. 25°. et Francie 2°. (Chartæ Antiquæ R. 227.) Archiv. Cantuar. Ecclesia S[ti]. Petri Cantuar. solvit annuam pensionem 6 sol. 8 den. Thesaurar. Cantuar. Registr. Henrici Prioris Cantuar. ab A. D. 1285. ad A. D. 1327. MS. in the Publick Library at Cambridge, marked E. e. v. fol. 31.

Charta Richardi de Langedone concedens Thomæ Personæ S[ti]. Petri Cant. et Successoribus suis, unum messuagium, cum pertinen. suis ecclesiæ S[ti]. Petri contiguum. Dat. 26 Sept. ann. regni Reg. Edw[di]. III. 27°. (Chartæ Antiquæ, A. 209.) Ibid.

Arbitratio facta a Nat. Brent, Mil. LL.D. de 13 sols. & 4 den. annuatim solvendis Rectori Eccl. S[ti]. Petri Cant. pro Decimis cujusdam Prati juxta

CANTERBURY.

juxta Situm Domus Fratrum minorum. Dat. 22 April, A. D. 1636. (Chartæ Antiquæ. A. 192) Ibid.

CHALLOCK, Chapel to Godmerſham.
Augmented by Archbiſhop Juxon 10l. per ann. By Indenture, 22 Aug. 13 Car. II. and another dat. 30 Dec. 23 Car. II. (L. L.)

CHARLTON, Rect.
Memorand. de Decimis Rect. de Cherlton. Leiger Book of St. Martin at Dover, fol. 253. b. (MSS. Lambeth.)

CHART, juxta Sutton, Vic.
Appropriatio dict. Eccl. Prior. et Convent. de Ledis per Walter Cant. Archiepum. Dat. apud Lambeth, 11 Kal. Aug. A. D. 1330, Reg. Reynolds, fol. 96. a 97. b. (Printed in Dr. Thorpe's Regiſtrum Roffenſe, p. 207, 208, 209.)

CHART MAGNA, Rect.

. Several Bounders of certain lands belonging to the Dean and Chapter of Canterbury, and lying in the Parish of Great Chart, being old Copies of three Indentures, one dated 23 Sept. 34 Hen. VIII. another dated 20 June, 4 Jac. I. another made by the Tenants of the said Lands, dated 29 Oct. 1614. Chartæ Miscellaneæ, vol. VI. N° 64. (MSS. Lambeth) Compositio inter mag. Reginald de London, Rect. Eccl. de Charte, ex una parte, et Prior. et Convent. S. Gregorii, Cantuar. ex altera super quibusdam Decimis, &c. Act. A. D. 1238, mense Decembri MS. in the Publick Library at Cambridge, marked Ll.—11—15 fol. 66.

Certificat Nichol. Decani et Capituli de Meideftane, quod Chart est Matrix Ecclesia, et non Capella de Sut-

Suttune. (Chartæ antiquæ Z. 54.) Archiv. Cantuar.

Dotatio Vicariæ de Chertæ juxta Ledes, per Walter. Archiep. Cant. apud Lambeth, 4 Kal. Marcii, A. D. 1320. (Chartæ Antiquæ, Z. 75.) Ibid.

Sententia de confuetudine et modo decimandi infra parochiam de Chart, Decanatus de Sutton, per Thomam Archiepifcopum Cant. lata in Caufa Decimarum, inter Priorem et Convent. de Ledes, et Johannem Hadde, parochianum dictæ ecclefiæ. Dat. apud Cranebrok, 1 die Julii, A. D. 1400. (Chartæ Antiquæ, Z. 76.) Ibid.

CHARTHAM, Rect.

Compofitio fuper quibufdam decimis redditibus poffeffionibus et rebus aliis inter Prior. et Convent. S. Gregorii Cant. et Mag. Robert. rectorem Eccl. de Charteham, Act. anno 1227 menfe Septembr. Chartæ et Conceffiones

DIOCESE OF

factæ Canonicis S. Gregorii Cantuar. MS. in the publick Library at Cambridge, marked Ll.—11—15. fol. 66.

CHISTELETT, Vic.

Ordinatio Vic. Dat. apud Lambeth, Id. Feb. A. D. 1345. Printed in X. Scriptores, col. 2115.

Augmented by Abp. Sheldon, 10l. per annum. By Indenture, dat. 13 July, 23 Car. II. (L. L.)

See a Compofition between the Abp. of Cant. and the Abbot of St. Auftin's, Cant. Dat. A. D. 1331. in which is an Account of the Endowment of this Vicarage. Regiftr. Album. (MSS. Lambeth.)

Copy of the Ordination of this Vicarage, and its prefent State (Temp. Sancroft) will be found at fol. 327. of a MS. of Abp. Sancroft, in the Bodleian

CANTERBURY. 25

· Bodleian Library, marked, m. p. Archp. S.

CLYVE S⁺ᵉ. MARGARETÆ, Vic.
Conventio fuper Decimis inter Vicarium Sᵗᵉ. Margaretæ de Clyve, et Sacriftam Dovorr. Dat. Cantuar. die Jovis in vigil. fefti B. Thomæ Apoftoli, A. D. 1296. (Leiger Book of the Priory of Sᵗ. Martin at Dover, fol. 144. a.) MSS. Lambeth. Augmented by Archbifhop Juxon, 26l. per ann. By Indenture, dat. 22 June, 13 Car. II. and another 21 July, 28 Car. II. (L. L)

COLREDE, Vic. See Ewell, al. Temple Ewell.
Confirmatio Capituli Eccl. Chrifti Cant. fuper Donatione Eccliar. de Apoldre et Colrede Prior. et Convent. Sʳⁱ. Martini de Dovorr.—Deductis inde competentibus vicariis, fcilicet in Eccl. de Apoldre vicaria xvi. Marcar.

Marcar. et in Eccl. de Colrede vicaria xii Marcar (fans Date.) Leiger Book of the Priory of S^t. Martin at Dover, fol. 187. b. (MSS. Lambeth.) Compofitio inter Abbat. et Convent. de Langedon et Prior. et Convent. S^{ti}. Martini de Dovorr. fuper Decimis de Popefhale infra Paroch. de Colrede — Facta autem fuit ifta Compofitio apud Cantuar. in Ecclefia Majori, in Natali Domini prox. poft confecrationem Hugonis Foliot, in Herfordenfem Epifcopum Pontificat. domini Honorii Pape tercii anno quarto (i. e. A. D. 1219.) Ibid. fol. 188. a.

Conventio facta inter Prior. et Convent S^{ti}. Martini de Dovorr. et Abbat. et Convent. de Langedon, fuper minutis decimis tenementi predicti Abbatis et Convent. quod tenent de Priore et Convent. de Cumb-

CANTERBURY. 27

Cumbwell in Paroch. de Colrede. Dat. in diem festi S^{ti}. Dionisii A. D. 1227. Ibid. fol. 188. b.

Supplicatio et Confirmatio Monachor. Cantuar. super Eccl. de Apoldre (sans Date.) Ibid. fol. 227. a.

Donatio Stephani (Langton) Cant. Archiep. et Cardinalis de Ecclesiis de Apoldre et Colrede Prior. et Convent. S^{ti}. Martini de Dovorr (sans Date.) Ibid.

Confirmatio Capituli Eccl. Christi Cant. super Donatione Eccliar. de Apoldre et Colrede (sans Date.) Ibid. fol. 227. b.

Collatio Eccl. de Apoldre reservata pensione Prior. et Convent. S^{ti}. Martini de Dovorr. (sans Date.) Ibid.

Alia Collatio Eccl. de Apoldre cum Capell. de Albeneia reservata pensione

sione x. solidor. Prior. et Convent. S^{ti}. Martini et Jure salvo (sans Date.) Ibid. fol. 228. a.

Transactio inter Ecclesias de Apoldre et Broclande super Decimis. Dat. apud Lameyam, A. D. 1203. dominica prox. ante fest. Sanctor. Fabiani et Sebestiani. Ibid. fol. 228. a.

Transactio inter personam de Broclande et Prior. et Convent. S^{ti}. Martini de Dovorr. super pensionibus, &c. pro Apoldre. Dat. in Eccl. Christi Cant. A. D. 1224. in Crastina Conversionis S^{ti}. Pauli. Ibid. fol. 228. b.

Diffinitiva Sententia contra Rectorem de Brokelonde pro Eccl. de Apoldre, super spoliatione 36 Corporum bladi, &c. Dat. Cant. 8 Id. Junii, A. D. 1318. Ibid. fol. 229. b.

Sen-

CANTERBURY. 29

Sententia pro Eccl. de Apoldre, pro Decimis contra Rectorem de Snargate (fans Date.) Ib. fol. 230. b.
Finalis concordia inter Prior. et Convent. S^{ti}. Martini de Dovorr. et Rectorem de Snargate, fuper Decimis. Dat. Men. Nov. in vigil S^{tæ}. Katerinæ, A. D. 1240. Ibid. fol. 231. a.
Compofitio inter Prior. et Convent. S$_{ti}$. Martini de Dovorr. et Rector. de Kenardyntone, fuper Decimis infra limites Eccl. de Apoldre et Kenardyntone. Dat. in Eccl. Chrifti Cant. Anno 2do poft tranflat. B. Thomæ Martiris. Ibid. fol. 231. b.
Compofitio inter Ecclefias de Apoldre et Kenardyntone fuper Decimis. Dat. 5 Id. Mart. A. D. 1228. Ibid. fol. 231. b.
Compofitio inter Abbat. et Convent. S^{ri}. Auguftini Cant. et Prior. et Convent.

vent. S_{ti}. Martini de Dovorr. super Decimis quarundam terrar. in Horinbroke et Sherle infra limites paroch. de Apoldre. Dat. mense Augusti, A. D. 1247. Ibid. fol. 232. b. Fines et limites Eccl. de Colrede cum capell. de Popleshale. Ibid. fol. 252. b.

Decretum Mag. Tho. de Cant. Commissar. Cantuar. generalis super quadam pensione vi. Marcar. Vicar. de Colrede debit. Dat. apud Lambeth, 18 Kal. Sept. A. D. 1346. Ibid. fol. 252. b. Inquisitio super pension. predict. Ibid. fol. 254. a. Augmented by Abp. Juxon 20l. per Ann. By Indenture, dat. 11 June, 14 Car. II. and another, 22 Mar. 22 Car. II.

Unio vicariarum de Sibertswell et Colrede. Dat. 13 die Feb. A. D. 1584.

1584. Reg. Whitgift, vol. I. fol. 459. (MSS. Lambeth.) Sententia Official. d'ni Archidiaconi Cantuar. lata inter Prior. et Convent. monaster. de Horton, et Johannem Rect. Eccl. de Snergate. super Decimis de Wytenewatfeld, de fabis seminat. Ibid. et de avenis. Dat. A. D. 1319. Die Lunæ prox. post dominicam qua cantatur officium misericordias domini (Registr. Priorat. de Horton, MS. hodie penes Tho. Astle, Arm. fol. 117, 118, 119. et fol. 149.)

Unio vicariarum de Sibertfwold, alias Shepherdswell et Colreade. Dat. 21 die April. A. D. 1680. Registr. Sancroft, fol. 384. a. b. (MSS. Lambeth.)

S. S. COSMI et DAMIANI, in le Blean, Vic.

Ordinatio Vicar. S. S. Cosmi et Damiani in le Blean—Decimæ apud Nat-

DIOCESE OF

Natyngdon. Onera Vicarii. Dat. apud Otteford, Non. Auguft. A. D. 1375. Reg. Sudbury, fol. 6. b. (MSS. Lambeth.) and printed in Somner's Ant. of Canterbury, 4to. London, 1640, in the Appendix, p. 399.

At Milkhoufe Street, in this parifh, was built, a little before the general Suppreffion of Religious Houfes, a Free Chapel (now in ruins) dedicated to the Holy Trinity, to which was given lands for its Endowment, which were valued at its Demolition at 84l. 7s. 10½d. per Annum, (which Lands were granted to Sir John Baker of Sifenhurft. (MS Lewis.)

CRANEBROKE, Vic.

Augmentatio portionis Vicar. de Cranebroke. Dat. 6 Id. Maii, A. D. 1364.—Reg. Iflip, fol. 201. b. Alia

CANTERBURY. 33

in Reg. Wittlefee, fol. 44. b. Dat. 4 Non. Junii, A. D. 1371. (MSS. Lambeth.)

Memorand. quod A. D. 1371, Richardus Prior et Convent. Ecclefiæ Chrifti Cant. confirmaverunt confirmationem Domini Will. Archiepif. fuper donationem * *Semonis* Archiepifcopi fui predecefforis de fex milibus de Tawod conceffis vicariæ de Cranebroke, de decimis Silvecedue, ad Ecclefiam de Cranebroke pertinent. (Reg. F. fol. 37. b.) MSS. Cantuar.

Commiffio in negotio moto inter Rectores de Bydindenne et de Cranebroke, fuper quibufdam limitibus ac jure parochiali et quibufdam aliis, directa G. de Middleton et Ric. de Stanhowe. Dat. apud Lameth, 7

* *Semonis*; fic Orig.

kal.

kal. Julii, A. D. 1314, Reg. Reynolds, fol. 9. b. (MSS. Lambeth.)

DEAL CHAPEL.

Built by Act of Parliament 9 Queen Anne, dedicated to St. George the Martyr, and confecrated by Abp. Wake in 1715. By the Act of Confecration, the Chapel Wardens are to allow to the Capellane 100l. per Annum. The faid Capellane to be nominated by the Archbifhop of Canterbury, who is Patron of the Mother Church. MS. Lewis.

DEBTLING, Vic.

Augmented by Archbifhop Juxon, 7l. 6s. 8d. per ann. befides the old penfion of 2l. 13s. 4d. By Indentures, dated 16 Aug. 13 Car. II. and 29 May, 27 Car. II. (L. L.)

Abp. Tenifon by his Will gave 2col. towards augmenting this poor Vicarage,

carage, which, together with Queen Anne's Bounty, has encreafed the Income 16l. per Annum.

Doddington, olim Dudintunia, Capella, hodie Vic.

A Penfion referved to it by Dr. Parker, Archdeacon of Canterbury, of 40l. per ann. by Leafe. Dat. 2 Aug. 27 Car. II. (L. L.)

Richardus (Wetherfhed) Cant. Archiepifcopus, &c. Noveritis quod dilectus filius et clericus nofter M. Girardus, cum effet perfona Ecclefiæ de Tenham, ad preces Hugonis filii Herevici, conceffit Capellæ de Dudintuniâ, ut Decimæ 20 acrarum de effarto de Pidinge, ad ufus Capellæ in perpetuum recipiantur, et per difpofitionem capellani, et 2 aut 3 parochianorum fidelium expendantur, ad fartatecta, libros, vefti-
menta,

menta, et ornamenta eidem Capellæ neceſſaria.—Nos autem hanc conceſſionem ratam habemus, &c. Teſtibus Will. Archidiacono Glo. et Moyſe Capellanis, M. Rogero de Rolveſton, &c. (Ex Archivis Eccl. Chriſti Cant. MS. Wharton, p. 61. N° 582. MSS. Lambeth.)

Dovor, S^{ti}. Jacobi, Rect.
Compoſitio inter Magiſtrum et Confratres Domus Dei, et Rector. S^{ti}. Jacobi Dovorr. ſuper jure percipiend. et habend. Decimas. Ibid. Dat. apud Lambeth, 16 die Maii, A. D. 1509. Reg. Warham, fol. 338. a, b. (MSS. Lambeth.) Abp. Teniſon gave 200l. towards augmenting this little Rectory.

EASTBREGGE, Eccl. (The Church demoliſhed.) See HOPE, near ROMNEY.

Con-

CANTERBURY.

Concerning the Tithes of this Parish, I have met with the following old Deeds; viz. "Processus inter Prior. "et Convent. de Horton et Rec- "torem Eccl. de Hope juxta Rom- "ney, de Decimis provenientibus de "terris dominicis Maneriorum de "Honeychild et Eastbrigge, ac etiam "de terris tenentium de feodo Ma- "nerior. predictor. in Marisco de "Romene existentibus in parochiis "Ecclesiarum de Hope et East- "brigge, A. D. 1310."

These Instruments, marked Chart. 180, 181, 182, 183, 184, 185, 186, and 187, are contained in the Register Book of the Priory of Horton in Kent, which MS. is now (1781) in the Library of Thomas Astle, Esq.)

Eastchurch, Vic.
Endowed with all the Tithes. Harris's Hift. of Kent, p. 108.

De conceffione undecim acr, et dim. Abbat. et Convent. de Dunis (Ciftercien. Ordinis) in Paroch. Eccl. de Eftcherch et conceffio VIII. fol. vicar. de Eftcherch et fuccefforibus fuis. Dat. A. D. 1300. fecundo die menfe Junii. (Augmentation Office, Chart. Mifcellaneæ, marked D. 99.)

Eastlangdon, Rect. et Northbourne, Vic.

Concordia facta inter Rectorem ecclefiæ de Eaft Langdon et Vicarium Eccl. parochial. de Northbourne, de annua folutione quatuor folid. dicto Vicario et fuis fuccefforibus, et confirmata per Abbat. et Convent. Mon. Beati Auguftini Cant. 1° die menfis April. A. D. 1396. In qua quid Charta parochiani ecclefiæ de Eaft-

CANTERBURY. 39

Eaftlangdon memorantur teneri, ad reparationem ecclefiæ de Northbourne. (Regift. R. fol. 31. a.) MS. Cantuar.

Confirmatio domini Will. Archiep. Cant. Dat. Cant. 3 April. A. D. fupradicto. (Ibid. fol. 31. b.)

Confirmatio Prior. et Capit. Cant. 4 April. A. D. fupradicto. (Ibid.)

EAST-SUTTON, Vic.

Augmented 24l. per ann. by Archbifhop Juxon. By Indentures, dat. 6 Mar. 13 Car. II. and 6 June, 26 Car. II. (L. L.)

EASTRY, Vic. See WOODNESBORNE.

Ordinatio Vicariæ. Dat. Kal. Sept. A. D. 1291.—Chartæ Mifcellaneæ, Vol. XI. N° 75. (MSS. Lambeth.)

Alia Ordinatio. Dat. 2 Non. Aug. A. D. 1367. Reg. Langham, fol. 129. b. (MSS. Lambeth.)

Compofitio inter Prior. et Capit.

Eccl. Chrifti Cant. et Anfelmum Rector. Eccl. de Eaftry fuper Decimis de Eaftry et Lyden, A. D. 1291. Chartular. Eccl. Chrifti Cant. Chart. 174.

Compofitio inter Rectorem de Eaftria, et Prior. et Convent. S^{ti}. Martini de Dovorr. fuper Decima de La Menefle, al. Worthe Mennefle. Act. A. D. 1229. Leiger Book of the Priory of St. Martin at Dover, fol. 164. b. (MSS. Lambeth.)

Confirmatio Richardi (Wetherfhed) Cant. Archiepifc. fuper Compofitione premiffa de Decima. Ibid. Dat. ut fupra.

Compofitio inter Priorem et Capit. Cantuar. et Vicarium ecclefiæ de Eaftry, de portione fua quam habebit in eadem. Confirmata per Simonem Cant. Archiepifcopum, apud le Forde, 2 Non. Augufti, A. D.

CANTERBURY.

A. D 1367. (Regift. Berthona, pars 1. fol. 39. a.) et Chartæ Antiquæ, E. 56. MS. Cantuar.

Fines et Limites Paroch. de Eaftry. (Chartæ Antiquæ, E. 113. 129. et Regift. Berthona, pars 1. fol. 46.) MSS. Cantuar. Finalis concordia inter Elemofinarium ecclefiæ Chrifti Cant. ac Thomam Vicarium ecclefiæ de Eaftry, fuper manfo Vicariæ, 5 Aug. A. D. 1368. (Chartæ Antiquæ, T. 132.) Archiv. Cantuar.

EASTRY, Vic. et B. MARIÆ SANDWICI, Vic.

Sententia in caufa Decimar. de terris in campo vocato Puttokfdowne, infra limites parochiæ de Eaftry provenientium. Inter Priorem et Convent. Cant. partem actricem et dominum Thomam, Vicarium ecclefiæ beatæ Mariæ de Sandwico, partem ream, ult. menfis Julii, A. D. 1439.

1439. (Chartæ Antiquæ, E. 133.) Archiv. Cantuar.

Sententia diffinitiva in caufa Decimar. provenientium de terris in campo vocato Puttokefdowne, inter Priorem et Capit. Cant. et Rectorem ecclefiæ de Eaftry ex parte una, et Vicar. ecclefiæ Beatæ Mariæ Sandwici ex altera parte, 16 Kal. Febr. A. D. 1346. (Reg. Berthona, pars 1. fol. 42, 43, 44, 45, 46, 47, 48, 49.) MSS. Cantuar.

Caufa Decimar. inter Priorem et Capit. Cant. et Will. de Cufington, Rector ecclefiæ de Eaftry, partem actricem, et dominum Richardum, Vicar. ecclefiæ Beatæ Mariæ Sandwici, partem ream, coram Auditore caufarum domini Cant. Archiepif. 10 Kal. Junii, A. D. 1356. (Chartæ Antiquæ, E. 129.) Archiv. Cantuar.

Ter-

CANTERBURY. 43

Terrarium de Worthe Meneffe fact. per 12 Jurat. de Hundred de Carvyle, anno 17 E. I. (Leiger Book of St. Martin at Dover, fol. 164. b. 165. a. (MSS. Lambeth.)

An Augmentation of 5l. 6s. 8d. is paid to the Vicar by the Dean and Chapter of Chrift Church, Canterbury, and 14l. 13s 4d. by the Leffee or Farmer of the Great Tithes. (MS. Lewis, p. 92.)

An Account of the Boundes and Lymites of this parifh, taken July 10, A. D. 1356, may be feen in a MS. marked A. 11. (fol. 68. b.) in the Archives of the Cathedral of Canterbury.

EGERTON Chapel, annexed to CHARING.

The Church of St. Paul in London, which is Patron, gave an Augmentation

tation to the Living of Egerton of 10l. per Ann. and the Parish bought also a Piece of Land in Stalesfeild, and applied it to the fame use; and the Berlings gave a House worth about 3l. per Ann. all which together amount to about 18l. per Ann. Dr. Harris's Hift. of Kent, p. 113.

ELHAM, Vic.
Compositio realis fact. per Archiepif. Cant. inter proprietar. de Elham, et Vicar. perpet. ibid. Codices Manuscripti Bibliothecæ Yelvertonianæ, N° 5251. Vol. XII. fol. 66. (Catal. MSS. Angliæ, part. II. p. 126.)
Vide in Cartulario archiepiscopatus Cantuar. (MS. Tanner in Bibl. Bodl. Oxon.) p. 97. Appropriationem Eccl. parochial. de Elham per Bonifacium Cant. Archiep. ad relevamen paupertatis et augmentum numeri Scholarium

CANTERBURY. 45

larium de Merton apud Meudon. Dat. 12 Kal. Maii, A. D. 1268. Elham (given to Merton College by Prince Edward, afterwards King Edward I.) had a vicarage of 30 marks per Ann. referved to it in Abp. Boniface's appropriation of it, bearing date 12 Kal. Maii, 1268. These 30 Marks as a stated Salary or Portion (and not Tithes, &c. to that Amount) were continued by a subsequent Composition or Decree of Abp. Wareham, bearing date 25 June, 1532, upon a Dispute between the College and Mr. John Webb, then Vicar of Elham, concerning the same. But in 1559 the College, of their own accord, agreed to let the Vicarial Tithes, &c. to Mr. Thomas Carden, the then Vicar, at an easy Rent, upon his discharging the said College of the sum of

6   20l.

20l. (al. 30 Marks) which they should " yearly pay to the vicar of " Elham, by virtue of the aforesaid " Composition." And this Lease, with this Clause or Condition, has been renewed to every subsequent Vicar since that Time. The Vicars now have likewise another Lease of some Wood-ground from the said College. See the original Instruments in the Treasury of Merton College.

Confirmatio Ade Prioris ecclesiæ Christi Cant. et ejusdem loci Conventus super carta Bonefacii Archiepisc. Cant. de ordinatione ecclesiæ de Elham, salva Vicaria xxx marcar. per Archiepisc. ordinand. Dat. apud Cant. in festo S^{ti}. Augstini Angl. primi doctoris, A. D. 1268. (Regist. G. fol. 509. a.) MSS. Cantuar.

CANTERBURY.

ELMSTEDE, Vic. See LYNTON.

Augmented in 1662 by Abp. Juxon, 10l. per Ann. besides the old Stipend of 10l. by Indenture, 11 July, 13 Car. II. (L. L.) Taxatio Vicariæ. Black Book of the Archdeacon of Canterbury, fol.—Ordinatio Vicariæ.—Leiger Book of the Priory of St. Gregory, by Canterbury.—Bp. More's Library at Cambridge.

EWELL, al. TEMPLE EWELL, Vic.

Terræ de quibus Decimæ solvuntur Manerio de Temple, sive Eccl. de Ewelle, infra limites paroch. de Colrede. Leiger Book of S^r. Martin at Dover, fol. 251. b. (MSS. Lambeth.)

EYTHORN, Vic.

Vide in Cartulario Archiepiscopopatus Cantuar. MS. in Bibl. Bodl. Oxon. inter libros MS. D'ni Tho. Tanner nuper Assaphen, Ep'i. p. 103. Ordinationem Stephani Archiepiscopi

piscopi Cantuar. pro tribus marcis annuatim solvendis monialibus de Harwolde, al. Harwood (Co. Bedford) a vicario Eccl. S. Petri de Egethorn et quietum clameum prioriſſæ et conventus factum Archiepiscopo Cantuar. et succeſſoribus de toto jure suo in dicta ecclesia de Egethorn quam habuerunt ex do ͦ Radulfi Morin.

FAIRFEILD Curacy.

The Curate's Stipend is 50l. per Ann. payable by the Farmer or Leſſee of the Manor.

FAWKENHERST, Rect. See **BONINGTON**.

FEVERSHAM, Vic.

Ordinatio Vicariæ (printed in Lewis's History of Feverſham Abbey, Appendix, N° XI. p. 50. and in X. Scriptores, col. 2091.)

Ordi-

CANTERBURY.

Ordinatio Vicariæ per Johannem Cant. Archiepifc. Dat. apud Lambeth, 8 Id. Mart. A. D. 1305. Register of St. Auftin of Cant. called the Blacke Boke, MS. in the Cotton Library (now in the Britifh Mufeum) marked Fauftina, A. 1. fol. 230. a, b. 231. a.

A long Paper Roll endorfed, *The Platt of Feverfham*—it is coloured — the various Places from the Town, viz. Houfes, Roads, Creeks, &c. down to Margate Road, are written down.—Records in the Cotton Library, not entered in the Cotton Catalogue (now in the Britifh Mufeum) marked XIII. 12.

FOLKSTONE, Vic.

Compofitio inter Priorat. de Folkeftone et Vicar. de Folkeftone fact. per Joh. Stafford Cant. Archiep. fuper porcione dict. Vicar. Dat. apud

apud Lameth 14 Junii, 1448. Reg. Stafford, fol. 29. b. 30. a. (MSS. Lambeth.)

Augmented by Archbishop Juxon 70l. per ann. besides the old Pension of 20l. By Indentures, 2 Nov. 13 Car. II. another 18 Aug. 26 Car. II. and another 17 April, 28 Car. II. (L. L.)

The West End of the Church of Folkestone was blown down on the 19th of Dec. 1705, and together with it two Arches of the Body of the Church, which consisted while standing of four Arches, one whereof, viz. that at the West End, hath always been useless, none of the Congregation ever sitting there, nor any Pews or Seats erected there; and forasmuch as in all probability the Clift on which it is built, constantly falling away, and the Sea gaining ground,

ground, within fifty years or less the whole Building will be utterly cast down and destroyed; the Curate and Inhabitants petitioned Abp. Tenison for leave to shorten the Church by rebuilding only one of the two fallen Arches, which was granted, 20 May, 1706.

GODMERSHAM, Vic.

Charta Hugonis de Mortuo Mari Rectoris ecclesie de Godmersham, de decimis minoribus non petendis ex manerio Prioris et Capit. Cant. de Godmersham provenientibus salvo jure successor. A. D. 1254. (Chartæ Antiquæ, C. 439. Archiv. Cantuar.) Dotatio Vicariæ de Godmersham, per Simon. Cant. Archiepisc. Dat. apud Bocton subtus le Blen, 8vo Kal. Octob. A. D. 1330. (Regist. Berthona. par. 1. fol. 225. a. MSS. Cantuar.)

DIOCESE OF

GODWYNESTON, Vic. hodie Cur. See NONINTON.

GOUDHERST, Vic.

Dotatio Vicariæ de Goudherſt, per Johannem Stretford, Archiepiſc. Cant. Dat. Cant. 4 April, 1341. Exemplificata per Will. Archiepiſc. Cant. apud Slyndon, 9 Febr. A. D. 1391. (Chartæ Antiquæ, A. 187.) Archiv. Cantuar.
Compoſitio Vicariæ, A. D. 1341. Reg. Spirit. Roffen. F. fol. 65. a. (In the Regiſtry of the Biſhop of Rocheſter, at Rocheſter.) Sententia Roberti Cant. Archiep'i ſuper Decimis Eccl. de Goutherſt Dat. apud Chartham, 6 Non. Maii, A. D. 1297. Reg. Winchelſea, fol. 212. b. (MSS. Lambeth.)

GRAVENEY, Vic.

It appears by an old Manuſcript formerly belonging to the Priory of St.

CANTERBURY. 53

St. Mary Overy in Southwark, that A. D. 1283. a Compofition for Tithe for the Vicarage of Graveney, was determined before the Dean of Ofpringe. Dr. Harris's Hift. of Kent, p. 227.

A Copy of this Compofition (Dat. die Lunæ, prox. ante feftum Apoftolor. Simonis et Judæ, A. D. 1283. e libro antiquo MS. quondam ad Prior. et Convent. S. Mariæ Overy in Southwark pertinent. fol. 192.) is preferved in MS. Lewis at Lambeth, p. 223.

GUSSITONA, hodie GUSTON, Vic. See CLYVE S_{tæ}. MARGARETÆ.

Appropriatio ecclefiæ de Gufiftona Prior. et Convent. Dovorr. per dominum Edmundum Archiepifc. falvis vicario viii. marc. Dat. apud Wingham, 5 Kal. Mart, A. D. 1239.   Chart.

Chart. Miscell. in Biblioth. Lambethana, Vol. V. N° 8.

Appropriatio Eccl. de Guchistone, al. Gostone, Prior. et Convent. S^{ti}. Martini Dovorr. per S^{tum}. Edmundum Cant. Archiepisc.—Salvis Vicar. viii. marc.—Dat. apud Wyngeham, 10 Kal. Maii, Pontificat. nostri anno 4. (i. e. A. D. 1239.) Leiger Book of the Priory of St. Martin at Dover, fol. 121. a. (MSS. Lambeth.)

Appropriatio Eccl. de Gostone per Gregorium Papam. Dat. Lateran. 12 Kal. Martii, Pontificat. nostri anno 7.

Compositio super quibusdam Decimis apud Gostone, contra Prior. et Convent. de Cumbewelle. Dat. apud Cumbewelle, 10 Kal. Junii, A. D. 1247. (Ibid.)

Descriptio limitum et finium Eccl.

Pa-

CANTERBURY. 55

Parochial. de Gofton, A. D. 1331. Ibid. fol. 254. a.

Augmented by Archbifhop Juxon 10l. per Ann. By Indentures, 10 July, 13 Car. II. and another 16 June, 27 Car. II. (L. L.)

HACKINGTON, Vic.

Augmentatio Vicariæ. Dat. 13 die Dec. A. D. 1588. Regift. Whitgift, pars 1ma. fol. 149. b. fol. 480. a, b. 481. a. (MSS. Lambeth.)

This Vicarage was augmented with the Tithes of Corn and Hay, paying 10l. yearly to the Archdeacon. Strype's Life of Archbifhop Whitgift, p. 284.

Augmentatio Vicariæ de Hackington, per Johannem Archiepif. Cant. cum confenfu Archidiaconi Cant. proprietarii Rectoriæ de Hackington, jure

jure fui Archidiaconatus. Dat. apud Lambeth, 13 Decemb. A. D. 1588. (Reg.W. fol. 248. a.) MSS. Cantuar. Confirmatio Decani et Capit. Cant. ult. Decemb. A. D. 1594. (Ibid. fol. 249. a.)

HALSTOWE, Vic.
Petition prefented to Archbifhop Tenifon by John White, Vicar of Halftow, fetting forth, That he has two Vicarage Houfes belonging to his Vicarage; one an old uninhabited Houfe adjoining to the Sea Side, that every Spring-Tide overflows with Salt Water, and which the Seamen and others have in a manner demolifhed; and that Part of it which is now ftanding, the Salt Water hath rotted the Timber, infomuch that it is not only altogether become ufelefs, but very

likely

CANTERBURY.

likely to become destructive to Cattle, that come often under it for shelter. The other is a House given by two Maids who died there, and bequeathed it to the Vicar for ever (in which he has inhabited twenty Years) the which was recovered by his Predecessor by due Course of Law. — Praying the Archbishop's Licence to demolish the former, in regard the Vicarage is small, not being worth 30l. per Ann.

The Archbishop's Licence for that purpose, dated 29 Octob. 1696. Reg. Tenison, part. 1. fol. 110. b. 111. a. (MSS. Lambeth.)

Charta Huberti Cant. Archiepisc. de ecclesia de Halegheſtowe, et reservatio pensionis annue Vicario ejusdem ecclesiæ. (Regiſt. C. fol. 32. a.) MSS. Cantuar.

Exemp-

Exemplificatio et confirmatio appropriationis ecclesiæ de Halegheſtow, reſervata penſione v. marcar. Vicar. ejuſdem, per Steph. Archiepiſc. Cant. Dat. apud Wingh. Idibus Novemb. anno primo ſolutionis interdicti Angl. generalis. (Chartæ Antiquæ, H. 100. Regiſtratur in libro G. fol. 105. b. et lib. C. fol. 31. a.) MSS. Cantuar.

Charta Bonefaci Archiepiſc. Cant. exemplificans et confirmans Chartam Huberti Archiepiſ. Cant. concedent. eccleſiam de Halegheſtow Prior. et Convent. Cant. ad emendationem librarii eccleſiæ Cant. ſalva Vicar. v. marcar. Dat. apud Liminge, A. D. 1266. menſ. Mart. (Chartæ Antiquæ G. 194. Regiſtratur in libro G. fol. 110. b.) Archiv. Cantuar.

Similis confirmatio, ſalva predicta Vicar. v. marcar. per Johannem

Ar-

CANTERBURY. 59

Archiepifc. Cant. apud Aldington, 10 Kal. Octob. 1282. Chartæ Antiquæ, G. 195.) Ibid.

HARDRES, Rect.

Sententia pro penfione 40 folid. contra Rectorem de Hardres coram official. D'ni Archidiaconi Cantuar. Dat. 13 Kal. Jan. A. D. 1312. Regiftr. Priorat. de Merton, fol. 183. Cleopatra C. VII. 20. in Bibl. Cotton. (In the Britifh Mufeum.)

HASTINGLEY, Rect.

Inhibitio verfus Rectorem de Haftinglegh per Commiffar. Cantuar. Dat. Cant. 3 Kal. Auguft. A. D. 1300. Proceffus Decimarum de Haftinglegh inter Prior. et Convent. de Horton et Rectorem de Haftinglegh, A. D. 1300. (Regiftr. Priorat. de Horton penes Tho. Aftle, Arm. fol. 115, 116, 117.)

HAWK-

HAWKHERST, Rect.

Dr. Harris in his Hist. of Kent, p. 148. gives an Account of the manner of paying Tithes here, taken from Kilburn. See also Magna Britannia et Hibernia, Vol. II. p. 1140. Decretum domini Geo. Abbott Cant. Archiepis. in causa taxationis ad reparationem Eccl. paroch. de Hawkeherst. Dat. apud Lambeth, 11 die Feb. A. D. 1631. Reg. Abbott. pars 3^{ia}. fol. 121. a, b.

Archbishop Abbot's Decision in a Cause concerning a Church *Seate* at Hawkherst, 23 Feb. A. D. 1631. (Chartæ Antiquæ, A. 76.) Archiv. Cantuar.

HAWKING, al. HAKINGE, Rect.

Abp. Tenison by his last Will gave 200l. towards the Augmentation of this little Church in his Patronage.

Hedcorn, Vic.

Augmentatio Vicar. de Hedcorne, facta A. D. 1267, per Magiftrum et fratres hofpitalis de Ofpring. In Cartulario Archiepif. Cant. inter MSS. Epif. Tanner in Bibl. Bodleiana Oxon. p. 99.

Herbledowne, Sti. Nicholai, Rect. Eadmundi Cant. Archiepifc. Exemplificatio et Confirmatio Compofitionis factæ inter Tho. Prior. et Convent. S^{ti}. Gregorii Cant. nomine ecclefiæ fuæ ex una parte, et Dom. Lucam Rectorem ecclefiæ de Herebaldun, nomine ecclefiæ fuæ ex altera, fuper quibufdam decimis infra parochiam de Herebaldun. Dat. apud . . . . Regiftrum antiquum cartarum et conceffionum factarum Canonicis S^{ti}. Gregorii Cantuar. fol. pergam. MS. non ita pridem in Bibl. R. R. P. D. D. Johannis Moore,

N° 283. nunc in Bibl. Public. Cantab. fol. 66. marked Ll. 11. 15.

In Batteley's Apppendix to Somner, p. 57. n. 29. I find Ecclefia S. Nicolai de Harbledoune in Decanatu Cant. among thofe which are exempt from the Archdeacon of Canterbury, and of confequence, as I prefume, fubject to the Commiffary.

The Tithes of this Church being appropriated to Eft-Bridge Hofpital, it is now no longer a prefentative Church, but ferves as a Chapel for the Hofpital there.

HERNE, Vic. See RECULVER.

Ordinatio Vicariæ. Dat. 3 Id. April, 1296. Reg. Winchelfee, fol. 185. b.

Exemplificatio dictæ ordinationis, 9 April, 1481. Reg. Bourghchier, fol. 100. b.

Alia exemplificatio dictæ ordinationis, 17 Junii, 1598. Reg. Whitgift,

gift, p. 3. fol. 93. a, b. 94. a (MSS. Lambeth.)

Ordinatio Vicariæ in capella de Herne. Dat. 5 Kal. Aug. A. D. 1308. Reg. Winchelſee, fol. 30. a.

The manner of paying the ſmall Tithes in the Pariſh of Herne, according to a Note of the ſame, written by John Hunte, Curate there, dated Aug. 10, 1621, may be ſeen in MS. Lewis, p. 226.

HERNHILL, Vic.

An annual penſion of 13s. 4d. is paid to the Vicar by the Impropriator. Pro limitibus dictæ parochiæ, vide SEASALTER.

HOLLINGBOURN, Vic.

Compoſitio facta per dominum Henricum (Chicheley) Cant. Archiepiſc. inter Will. Lyeff Rectorem modernum, et Johannem Ffylde, Vicar. Eccl. paroch. de Holyngbourne,
ſnper

super jure requisit. ad ordinationem, limitationem, ac assignationem, dotis et portionis, quam in dict. Eccl. Vicar. predict. et successores sui perpetui futuris temporibus percipient et habebunt. (Sans Date, sed circa A. D. 1441.) Reg. Chicheley, pars 1ma. fol. 237. a, b. (MSS. Lambeth.) Concessio cujusdam messuagii cum pertinent. in Hollingbourn, facta per Arnold Sentleger, Arm. Will. Maunby, Vicar. de Hollingbourn, pro inhabitatione ipsius Will. et successorum suorum in perpetuum. Dat. apud Hollingbourn, 14 die Aug. A. D. 1407. Reg. Chicheley, pars 1ma. fol. 238. a. (MSS. Lambeth.)

HOPE, juxta ROMNEY, Rect.

Processus inter Prior. et Convent. de Horton et Rectorem Eccl. Omnium Sanctorum de Hope juxta Romene de Decimis provenient. de terris dominicis

CANTERBURY. 65
minicis maneriorum de Honeychild et Eftbrigge, ac etiam de terris tenentium de feodo maneriorum predictorum in Marifco de Romene exiftentibus in parochiis Ecclefiarum de Hope et Eftbregge, A. D. 1310. Regiftr. Priorat. de Horton. Chart. 180. ad Chart. 187. (MS. hodie, A. D. 1781, penes Tho. Aftle, Arm.)
HOLLINGBORNE, Vic.
Compofitio facta per dominum Henricum (Chicheley) Cant. Archiepifc. inter Will. Lyeff Rectorem modernum, et Johannem Ffylde, Vicar. Eccl. paroch. de Holyngbourne, fuper jure requifit. ad ordinationem, limitationem, ac affignationem, dotis et portionis, quam in dict. Eccl. Vicar. predict. et fucceffores fui perpetui futuris temporibus percipient et habebunt. (Sans Date, fed circa A. D. 1441.)

DIOCESE OF

1441.) Reg. Chicheley, pars 1ma. fol. 257. a, b. (MSS. Lambeth.)

Conceffio cujufdam meffuagii cum pertinent. in Hollingbourn, facta per Arnold Sentleger, Arm. Will. Maunby, Vicar. de Hollingbourn, pro inhabitatione ipfius Will. et fuccefforum fuorum in perpetuum. Dat. apud Hollingbourn, 14 die Aug. A. D. 1407. Reg. Chicheley, pars 1ma. fol. 238. a. (MSS. Lambeth.) Augmented 20l. per Ann. by Leafe, dated Feb. 2, 1682, between Ralph Staunton Rector of Hollingbourn, and Sir Tho. Culpepper of Hollingbourne, Knt. (L. L.)

HONEYCHILD MANOR. See HOPE near ROMNEY.

HOTHE, Capella.

Inhabitantes ibid. tenentur ad reparationes ecclefiæ de Reculver, fecundum ordinationem Thomæ Archiepifc.

chiepifc. Cant. Dat. apud Ford, 20 Januar. A. D. 1410. (Chartæ Antiquæ, C. 188. Archiv. Cantuar.)
HOUGHAM, olim HUGHAM, Vic.
Ordinatio Johannis (Stratford) Cant. Archiepifc. fuper Vicaria in ecclefia de Hugham, et de fingulis proventibus ipfius per Vicarium percipiendis. Dat. apud Maghffeld, 13 Kal. Jan. A. D. 1345. et noftre tranflationis duodecimo. Leiger Book of the Priory of St Martin at Dover, fol. 194. b. (MSS. Lambeth.)
N. B. The Regifter Book of Archbifhop Stratford having been loft for feveral hundred Years, the Endowment of Hougham is happily preferved in this Leiger Book of St. Martin at Dover, to which it was appropriated. Hougham was augmented 25l. by Archbifhop Juxon. By Indentures, dat. 24 Feb. 14 Car. II.

II. and another, dat. 25 July, 22 Car. II. (L. L.)

Abp. Tenifon, by his laft Will, left 200l. towards the Augmentation of this fmall Vicarage.

ST. JOHN BAPTIST in Thanet, Vic. Queen Mary's Letters Patent for the Augmentation of the Vicarage of St. John Baptift in Thanet. (dat. 6 die Nov. anno regni primo) is printed in Lewis's Hift. of the Ifle of Thanet. Coll. N° xxxv. p. 70. Edit. 1736.—Ibid. Coll. N° xxxvi. p. 72. A true Terrier of all the Glebe Lands belonging to the Vicarage of St. John Baptift in Thanet, made at the Command and Appointment of my Lord's Grace of Canterbury, in his Metropolitical Vifitation (A. D. 1615.) by the Churchwardens and Affiftants, fworn Men of the fame Parifh, who have
here-

CANTERBURY. 69

hereunto put their Hands; together with the Minister there, according to the Canon.

Commissio d'ni Simonis Cantuar. Archiepi. directa mag. Tho. Baketon, Canonico in Eccl. Lyncoln, et Will. Byde Canonico in Eccl. Sarum, in causa augmentationis dict. Vicariæ. Dat. apud Lambeth, 4 Id. Oct. A. D. 1375. Reg. Sudbury, fol. 9. a. (MSS. Lambeth.)

IWADE, al. WADE, Cur.

This Curacy was augmented 8l. per Annum by Lease, dat. 20 Feb. 1660, between Geo. Hall, D. D. Archdeacon of Canterbury, and Anne Lyne, Spinster, of Canterbury. (L. L.)

KENARTON, al. KENARDINGTON. See COLREDE.

DIOCESE OF

KENYNGTON, Vic.

Ordinatio Vicar. A. D. 1349. printed in X. Script. col. 2104. Ordinatio Vicar. per Johannem Cant. Archiepifc. (fans Date.) Regifter of St. Auftin, Cant. called the Blacke Boke, MS. in the Cotton Library (now in the Britifh Mufeum), marked Fauftina, A. 1. fol. 234. a, b.

Affignatio portionis vicarii. Dat. apud Lameth, 13 Kal. Jan. A. D. 1316. Reg. Reynolds, fol. 18. b. (MSS. Lambth.) Copia Compofitionis dict. Vicariæ extat in MS. notat. A. 11. fol. 38. in Archiv. Eccl. Cathedral. Cantuarienfis.

KYNGESNODE, Vic.

Ordinatio Vicar. Dat. 18 Kal. Julii, A. D. 1298. Reg. Winchelfea, fol. 271. b. (MSS. Lambeth.)

CANTERBURY.

STI. LAURENTII (in Thaneto) Vic.
See MENSTRE in Thaneto.

In 1660, in purſuance of the Royal Directions at that Time iſſued, Archbiſhop Juxon added to the poor Penſion, before paid to the Vicar out of Newland, an Augmentation of 40l. per ann. By Indenture, dat. 17 July, 13 Car. II. (L. L.)

LEEDS cum BROMFEILD, Cur.

In 1661, Abp. Juxon augmented this Curacy and Bromfeild out of the Great Tithes, 30l. per Ann. beſides the old Penſion of 22l. 6s. 8d. By Indentures, dat. 1 June, 13 Car. II. and one 17 April, 29 Car. II. (L.L.)

LENHAM, Vic.

Ordinatio Vicar. A. D. 1349. (printed in X. Script. col. 2098.)
Compoſitio Eccl. de Lenham. — Eadmund. Archiep'us Cant. &c. Omnes majores Decimæ quas Prior

et Convent. S. Gregorii ab antiquo de dominio de Henham percipiunt remaneant perpetuo et pacifice eifdem et omne jus minorum Decimar. et fepultor. defunctor. refignent. Actum A. D. 1240 menfe Julii. Chartæ et Conceffiones factæ Canonicis S^{ti}. Gregorii Cantuar. MS. in the Publick Library at Cambridge, marked Ll. 11. 15. fol. 66.—Copia Compoffitionis dict. Vicariæ per Edmund Cant. Archiep'um. Dat. apud Wingham, 10 Kal. Aug. Pont. fui anno 7. (i. e. A. D. 1241.) extat in MS. A. 11. fol. 92. b. in Archiv. Eccl. Cathedral. Cantuar.

LEYSDOWN in the Ifle of Shepey, Vic. Ordinatio Vicar. Eccl. S^{ti}. Radegundi de Bradfole, et Eccl. S^{ti}. Clementis Leyfdown in Scapeia, Act. 23 die Mart. A. D. 1223. N° 32. et N° 92. in Regift. Cantuar. temp. Henrici

CANTERBURY.

Henrici Prioris, a 4 die April. A. D. 1285. ad 21 die Nov. A. D. 1327.

LIDE, Vic.

Ordinatio Vicar. Dat. 10 Kal. Maii, A. D. 1321. Reg. Reynolds, fol. 102. b. (MSS. Lambeth.)
It appears by Abp. Reynolds's Register Book, fee fol. 200. a. 203. a. and 289. b. that in the year 1321 this Church was appropriated *Abbati et Convent. B. Marie de Gloria Avagnium Dioc. Floren. Ordinis*; and that the Collation of this Vicarage was referved to the Abp. of Cant. and his Succeffors.

LITTLEBURNE, Vic.

Ratihabitio Abbatis S[ti]. Auguftini Cantuar. de Ordinatione Vicar. ecclefiæ de Littleburne. (Printed in X. Script. col. 2106.) Conventio cum procuratore Abbat. Montis Mirteti fuper ecclefia predicta. Ibid. col. 2107. Or-

Ordinatio Vicar. Dat. 8 Id. Mart. A. D. 1345. Ibid. col. 2106.
Ordinatio Vicar. de Littleburne. Dat. apud Cherryng, 14 Kal. Aug. A. D. 1370. Ibid. col. 2108.
Taxatio Vicar de Littleburne. Dat. apud Egneſham, 12 Kal. Maii. Pont. domini Gregorii Pape noni anno 12. Red Book of Canterbury MS. in the Cotton Library (now in the Britiſh Muſeum) marked Claudius D. X. fol. 41. b. 42. a, b. 43. a.
Qualiter ſacerdos de Littleburne, debeat celebrare in capell. de Luke-dale (ſans Date.) Ibid. fol. 43. a.
Augmented 50l. per Ann. by the Dean and Chapter of Canterbury.

LIVINGEBURN. See BEAKISBOURN.
LOOSE CHAPEL.

Augmented 5l. 13s. 4d. by Indentures, dat. 16 Auguſt, 13 Car. I. and 20 May, 27 Car. II. (L. L.)

LYD-

LYDDEN, Vic. See EASTRY.

Augmented by Archbifhop Juxon 18l. per Ann. By Indenture, dated 2 May, 25. Car. II. (L. L.)

Abp. Tenifon left by his laft Will 200l. to augment this fmall Vicarage.

LYNSTED, Vic.

A Penfion referved to it by Dr Parker, Archdeacon of Canterbury, of 10l. per Ann. by Leafe. Dat. 2 Aug. 27 Car. II.

LYNTON, Vic.

Copia Compofitionis Vicariar. de Lynton et Elmfted extat in MS. A. 11. in Archiv. Eccl. Cathedral. Cantuar.

Compofitio facta per dominum Matthæum (Parker) Cant. Archiepifc. inter proprietarium et parochianos de Lillington, al. Lynton, fuper affignatione et admiffione unius Capellani

DIOCESE OF

lani idonei ad deferviend. curæ dict. parochiæ in divinis et aliis requifitis, &c. et de et fuper affignatione et limitatione porcionis congrue et competent. eidem capellano. Dat. 12 Junii, A. D 1562. Reg. Parker, pars 1ma. fol. 356. a, b. 357. a (MSS. Lambeth.)

MAIDSTONE, Curacy,

Was firft augmented ten pounds per Annum by Abp Whitgift. (See an Account of this Curacy in Newton's Hiftory of Maidftone, p. 58. 8vo. London, 1741.) Afterwards it was augmented 37l. 6s 8d. beyond the former Penfion of 20l. by Archbifhop Juxon. By Indentures, dat. 16 Aug. 13 Car. I. and 29 May, 27 Car. II. (L. L.)

Archbifhop Sancroft, by Leafe, dated July 10, 1677, gave to the Curate of Maidftone, for Augmentation of his

CANTERBURY. 77

his Maintenance in Supply of that Cure, "all the small Tithes of the Boroughs or Towns of Week and Stone within the said Parish, all the Commodities of the Church-yard of Maidstone, and one Moiety of the small Tithes within the Town or Borough of Maidstone." (L. L.)

MARDEN, Vic.

Copia Ordinationis dict. vicariæ appropriat. Monaster. de Lesnes. Dat. apud Maghfeld, 12 Kal. April, A. D. 1341. extat in MS. notat. A. 11. fol. 70. in Archiv. Eccl. Cathedral Cantuariensis.

Augmented by Archbishop Juxon 20l. per ann. By Indenture, dated 28 May, 15 Car. II. (L. L.)

MENSTRE, Vic.

De dotatione Eccl. de Menstre cum
Ca-

Capellis (printed in X. Script. col. 2116.)

Confirmatio Pape super eadem. Ibid. col. 2117.

Confirmatio Theobaldi Cant. Archiepisc. de eadem. Ibid. 2117.

Compositio inter Vicarium de Menstre, et Vicarium S^{ti}. Laurentii in Thaneto. Dat. in crastino nativitatis B. Mariæ, A. D. 1275. (printed in X. Script. col. 1922.)

Concerning the Tithes of this Vicarage, see Lewis's Hist. of the Isle of Thanet, p. 99, et seq. Edit. 1736. See also ibid. Coll. N° XXVII. p. 44.

A Terrier of the Parsonage and Vicarage of Minster in Thanet, Dat. Sept. 11, 1615.

Compositio facta inter Matricem Eccl. de Menstre et Capellam S^{ti}. Laurentii in Thaneto, sub sigillo domini Roberti

CANTERBURY.

berti (Kilwarby) Cant. Archiepifc. et Capituli S^{ti}. Auguftini Cantuar. ac Vicarior. de Menftre et S^{ti}. Laurentii, fuper fepultura mortuorum, ac decimis, oblationibus, et diverfis aliis. Dat. Cantuar. 4 Kal. Junii, A. D. 1278. Red Book of Canterbury MS. in the Cotton Library (now in the Britifh Mufeum) marked Claudius D. X. fol. 323. a, b.
Ordinatio Vicarie et Capellar. S. Petri, Johannis, et Laurentii, extat in Regiftro Albo, in quadam Compofitione inter Archiep. Cantuar. et Abbat. S^{ti}. Auguftini Cant. dat. A. D. 1331. (MSS. Lambeth.)

MIDLEY, Rect. See ROMENAL.

MIDDLETON, Vic.

Ordinatio Vicar. de Middleton extat apud Chartas Antiquas Eccl. Chrifti Cantüar. (printed in X. Script. col. 2093.)

Or-

Ordinatio Vicar. per Johannem (Stratford) Cant. Archiepifc. Dat. apud Lambeth, 8 Id. Mart. A. D. 1345. Regifter of St. Auftin, Cant. called the Blacke Boke, MS. in the Cotton Library (now in the Britifh Mufeum) marked Fauftina A. 1. fol. 231. b.

MILTON, juxta Sittingbourn, Vic.

Charta Roberti de Wikes Vicar. de Middleton, de 7 Deywercis terræ, cum domibus defuper factis, pro inhabitatione Vicarii de Middleton, qui pro tempore fuerit. Dat. Cant. A. D. 1247, 27 Maii. (Chartæ Antiquæ, I. 49.) Archiv. Cantuar.

Portio Vicar. de Middleton affignata per Abbat. et Convent. S^{ti}. Auguftini, 6 Non. Martii, A. D. 1286. (Chatæ Antiquæ I. 54.) Ibid.

MONKETON, Vic.

Ordinatio Vicariæ. Dat. 2 Non. Auguft,

guſt, A. D. 1367. Regiſt. Langham, fol. 130. b. (MSS. Lambeth.) Extat in Regiſt. Eccl. Chriſti Cant.—Printed in Lewis's Hiſt. of the Iſle of Thanet, Coll. IX. p. 16.

A Terrier of the Houſes and Glebe Land belonging unto the Vicarage of Monketon in the Iſle of Thanet, taken July 7, 1630, is printed in Lewis's Hiſt. of the Iſle of Thanet, Coll. N° XI, XII. p. 17, 18.

Compoſitio inter Prior. et Capit. Cant. et Vicar. eccleſiæ de Monketon, de portione ſua quam habebit in eadem. Confirmata per Simonem Archiepiſc. Cant. apud le Forde, 2 Non. Auguſt. A. D 1367. (Reg. Berthona, pars 1. fol. 144. b.) MSS. Cantuar.

NACKINGTON, hodie Cur. olim Vic.
Inquiſitio de vicaria de Nacindon.—Regiſtr. Henrici Prioris Cantuar. MS.

MS. in the Publick Library at Cambridge, marked Ee, v. fol. 37. — An Account of the Bounds and Limits of this Parish (without Date) is extant in MS. A. 11. fol. 93. a. in the Archives of Canterbury Cathedral. This Curacy was augmented 20l. per Ann. by Indenture, dated 17 April, 28 Car. II. (L. L.)

NEWCHURCHE, Vic.
Ordinatio Vicar. Dat. 3 Kal. Junii, A. D. 1297.—Reg. Winchelsea, fol. 214. b. (MSS. Lambeth.)
Alia Ordinatio Dat. apud Maydeston, 22 die mensis Maii, A. D. 1404. Reg. Arundel, pars 1ma. fol. 350. b. (MSS. Lambeth.)

NEWENDEN, Rect.
Petition presented to Archbishop Tenison, by the Inhabitants and Occupiers of Land in the Parish of New-

CANTERBURY. 83

Newenden, setting forth the ruinous Condition of the Steeple and Chancel of the said Parish; and desiring his Leave that the said Steeple and Chancel may be wholly taken away, and the Body of the Church only put into good Repair, and a Turret built upon the Top of the same to hang up one of the Bells in; and that the other two Bells belonging to the Church, with the Materials of Timber and Stone which shall remain, after the Repairs of the Body of the Church are compleated, may be sold.—The Archbishop's Faculty for that Purpose, dated April 1, 1700. Reg. Tenison, part 1. fol. 128. a, b. (MSS. Lambeth.)

NEWINGTON, Vic.

Ordinatio Walteri Cant. Archiep'i super decimis de la Dene et Hildestede inter parochianos de Newington et Stokbyr Cant. Dioc. Dat. apud Lambeth die Lune prox. poft Feft. S^{ti}. Edmundi, A. D. 1324. Regiftr. Vet. Cartar. Convent. Eccl. Chrifti Cant. fol. 253. (In Bp. Moore's Library at Cambridge.)

NEWSOLE CAPELLA.

Terræ de quibus Abbas de Langedon percipiet decimas majores et minores, racione Capelle de Newefole (fans Date) Leiger Book of the Priory of St. Martin at Dover, fol. 155. a. (MSS. Lambeth.)

STI. NICOLAI et OMNIUM SANCTOR. Capellæ in Thaneto.

Ordinatio domini Johannis Peckham Cant. Archiepifc. inter parochianos Capellarum Omnium Sanctor. et S^{ti}. Nicolai in Thaneto. Dat. apud Aldyngton, 5 Kal. Maii, A. D. 1284. Reg. Peckham, fol. 206. b. (MSS. Lambeth.)

CANTERBURY.

Inquifitio fuper finibus parochiar. S^{ti}. Nicolai et Omnium Sanctor. de Capell. Infulæ de Taneto, et matrice Eccl. de Reculver dependentium. Dat. 2 Id. Mart. A. D. 1297. Reg. Winchelfea, fol. 240. a. (MSS. Lambeth)

Ordinatio ftrate pertinentis ad Capellam Omnium Sanctorum in Thaneto. Ibid. fol. 193. a.

Ordinatio vicariæ in Capella S^{ti}. Nicolai cum Capella Omnium Sanctorum annex. Dat. 5 Kal. Aug. A. D. 1308. Ibid. fol. 30. a.

Augmented 30l. per ann. by Indentures, dated 14 Aug. 13 Car. II. and another, dated 4 Jan. 20 Car. II. (L. L.)

A Terrier of the Glebe Land belonging to the Vicarage of St. Nicholas at Wade within the Ifle of Thanet, dated June 10, A. D. 1630,

1630, is printed in Lewis's Hift. of the Ifle of Thanet. Coll. N° IV. p. 4. Edit. 1736. See RECULVER. NONYNGTON, olim Vic. hodie Cur. Ordinatio Joh'is Peckham, Cant. Archiep. de divifione Eccl. de Wyngham in 4 prebendas, viz 1. Eccl. de Wyngham. 2. Paroch. de Effe cum capell de Flete. 3. Eccl. de Godwynefton. 4. Eccl. de Nonyngton, falvis fupradictis quibufdam porcionibus quas vicariis hactenus libere percipiffe nofcuntur. Dat. apud Wengham, 4 Non. Aug. A. D. 1282. Reg. Pecham, fol. 104. b. (MSS. Lambeth.)

Augmented by Archbifhop Juxon 20l. per ann. By Indentures, dat. 10 ec. 14 C. r. II. and another, dat. 10 Sept. 14 Car. II. (L. L.)

NORBORNE, Vic.
Ordinatio Vicar. circa A. D. 1349. (printed in X. Script. col. 2112.) See EASTLANGDON and NORTHBOURNE.

NORBORNE cum SHOULDEN, Vic.
Exemplar atteſtatum de dotatione Vicar. de Norborne et Shoulden a Johanne Archiepiſc. Cantuar. facta A. D. 1268. Id. Febr. (Chartæ Ant. N° 19. Archiv. Cantuar.)
Pro penſione 4 ſolid. debit. Vicar. Ibid. Vide EASTLANGDON.

OSTENHANGER, al. EASTINGHER, Rect.
The Church long ſince demoliſhed, and the Tithes a Lay Fee. It is now reputed to belong to the Pariſh of Stanford (in the Deanry of Elham) to which Chapel the few Inhabitants of this Pariſh reſort to hear Divine Service. There is paid
out

out of this Rectory to the adjoining Chapel of Stanford 10s. per ann. But, quære, how long? (MS. Lewis, p. 117.)

OTRINGDENNE, Vic.

Sententia diffinitiva Delegatorum Gregorii Pape. (Dat. 3 die Martii, Pont. fui Anno 5.) de Decimis omnium Multorum pofcentium in Dominico D'ni F. de Wappingborne infra Eccl. Paroch. de Otringdenne (Cant. Dioc.) in quadam Caufa litigat. inter Prior. et Convent. de Leawes et Eadmund Rect. Eccl. de Otringdenn. predict. (3 Deeds) at the Chapter Houfe, Weftminfter.

OVERLAND CHAPEL,

Has long fince been in ruins. Abp. Juxon, in whofe time poffibly the Chapel might be ftanding, augmented it 1cl. per ann. out of the Leafe of the Tithes, &c. By Indentures,

dentures, dat. 18 Nov. 13 Car. II. and one Aug. 2. 23 Car. II. (L. L.)
OWRE, al. OARE, Cur.
The Stipend of the Curate augmented 12l. by Indentures, one dat. 17 April, 28 Car. II. another, dat. 11 July, 13 Car. II. 12l. (L. L.)
PATRIKESBOURN, Vic.
Ordinatio et Appropriatio Eccl. de Patrikeſbourn Convent. de Merton. Dat. in Vigil. S^{ti}. Johannis Baptiſtæ A. D. 1258. Reg. Arundel, pars 1ma. fol. 15. a, b. (MSS. Lambeth.)
Inquiſitio de fructibus dict. Eccl. et Ordinatio vicariæ (ſans Date) Regiſtr. Priorat. de Merton, fol. 213. ad fol. 217. In Bibl. Cotton. (In the Britiſh Muſeum) marked Cleopatra, C. VII. 20.
ST. PETER in the Iſle of Thanet, Vic.
A Terrier of the Vicarage Houſe and of the Glebe Lands thereunto be-

belonging, of the Parifh of St. Peter the Apoftle, in the Ifle of Thanet, made and taken by the Churchwardens and Affiftants of the faid Parifh, the 22d of May, 1630, is printed in Lewis's Hift. of the Ifle of Thanet, Coll. XLVI. p. 92. where an Account of this Vicarage may be found.

PETHAM, Vic.

Affignatio portionis Vicarii. Dat. menfe Decembr. A. D. 1226. Reg. Warham, fol. 163. b. (MSS. Lambeth.) See WALTHAM and PETHAM.

PEVINGTON, Rect.

Decree of Archbifhop Abbot concerning the Tithes of Pevington. Dat. May 16, 1618. Reg. Abbot, pars 3ª. fol. 181 a, b.—N. B. In a Suit concerning the Tithes of this Parifh, (viz. Copley verf. Spice) it was

CANTERBURY. 91

was agreed to withdraw a Juryman, and to refer it to Archbifhop Abbot. Regift. Abbot, ibid. (MSS. Lambeth.) United to Pluckley, 28 Jan. A. D. 1583. Reg. Whitgift, vol. I. fol. 451. (MSS. Lambeth.)

PLUCKLEY, Rect. See PEVINGTON.
POPLESHALE, Capella. See COLREDE.
POSTLING, Vic.

See in Bifhop Kennet's Cafe of Impropriations, p. 306. a Leafe made of the Impropriate Rectory by Archbifhop Sancroft, for the Benefit of the Vicar of Poftling and his Succeffors. Dat. July 17, 1688. See alfo Dr. Harris's Hift. of Kent, p. 242.

PRESTON, juxta Wengham, Vic.

Ordinatio Vicar. A. D. 1349. (printed in the X. Script. col. 2109.) Appropriatio dict. Eccl. A. D. 1215. Kal. Aug. Regift. Warham, f. 96. a,

In

DIOCESE OF

In the year .... Wybourne gave to the Vicar of this Parish, and his Successors, on condition of their residing there, and performing Divine Service twice every Lord's Day, his Dwelling-house, with the Estate thereto belonging, valued at about 40 or 50 Pounds a Year, by which means this Vicarage is of the Value of about 100l. per ann. A Stipend of 3l. is paid to the Vicar out of the Exchequer by the Receiver General of the King's Tax for Kent. Tho. Watts, Vicar of this Parish, by his Will, dated Oct. 10, A. D. 1507, gave a Tenement in this Parish, with five Acres of Land, to the Churchwardens, on the following Conditions; viz. that they applied to the Use of the Church 4s. 8d. that they gave on the Day of his Anniversary to the Vicar 12 Pence, *pro labore*

labore ut oret pro anima mea in pulpeto; *Aquebajula* viiid. *et offeret* 1d. *et dabit* 3 *pauperibus* 3d. After the Reformation, this Houfe, &c. was infeofed in Truftees, and the Rents and Profits of it directed to be applied to the Repairs of the Church. (MS. Lewis, p. 132.)

RECULVER, Vic. See S^{ti}. NICOLAI et OMNIUM SANCTOR. Capellæ in Thaneto. See HOTHE, Capella.
Ordinatio Vicar. Dat. 3 Id. April. A. D. 1296. Reg. Winchelfea, fol. 185. b. (MSS. Lambeth.)—Alia Ordinatio. Dat. 5 Kal. Aug. A. D. 1308. Ibid. fol. 30. a.
Ordinatio inter Vicar. de Reculver et parochianos ejufdem fuper oblationibus, feu eleemofinis in quodam trunco juxta magnam crucem lapideam, inter ecclefiam et cancellam repofitis, &c. Dat. apud Reculver, 3 Id.

3 Id. April, A. D. 1296. Reg. Winchelſea fol. 185. b. (MSS. Lambeth.)

Ordinatio inter Vicar. Eccl. de Reculver in Capell. S^{ti}. Michaelis in Thaneto, in Capella de Hothe, et in Capella de Herne. Dat. apud Cheryng, 9 Kal. Aug. A. D. 1308. Reg. Bourchier, fol. 100. b. (MSS. Lambeth.)

Walteri Reynold. Cant. Archiep'i Ordinatio ſuper quibuſdam Decimis in parochia de Stourmouth ad Rectorem de Reculver pertinent. Dat. apud Lameth, 14 Kal. April, A. D. 1315. (The original Inſtrument is among the Chartæ Miſcellaneæ in the MS. Library at Lambeth, Vol. VI. N° 66.)

Exemplificatio antiqua continens varia Inſtrumenta ad Eccl. de Reculver et Herne ſpectant. (In all 9; the laſt

CANTERBURY. 95

laſt of which is dated 3 Dec. 1389). Among the Archives of the Dean and Chapter of Canterbury.—Concerning theſe Churches, ſee Somner's Treatiſe of the Roman Ports and Forts, 12mo, Oxon. 1693, p. 84.

Exemplificatio Ordinationis dictarum *trium* Vicar. per Johannem Parmenter, Commiſſar. General. Dat. 9 April, A. D. 1481. Reg. Bourgchier, fol. 100. b. (MSS. Lambeth.) Alia exemplificatio dictæ Ordinationis per Johannem Whitgift, Cant. Archiepiſc. Dat. 17 Junii, A. D. 1598. Reg. Whitgift, pars III. fol. 93. a. b. (MSS. Lambeth.)

Compoſitio inter Tho. Nightingale, Vicar. Eccl. parochial. et matricis de Reculver, Joh. Cocke et Joh. Cobbe, economos ſive bonorum cuſtodes Eccl. predict. et Mag. Hen. Holande, Vicar. capellæ S^{ti}. Nicolai in Thaneto, et Joh. Everard et Rob. Abraham, economos five bonorum cuftodes ejufdem capelle et parochianor. inhabitant. coram domino Will. (Warham) Cant. Archiepifc. de annua folutione 3s. 4d. et fuper confectione, et reparatione dicte matricis Eccl. Dat. apud Cant. 24 die Aug. A. D. 1528. Reg. Whitgift, pars 1ma. fol. 257. a, b. (MSS. Lambeth.)

Decree of Archbifhop Whitgift concerning the faid Compofition. Dat. Auguft 31, A. D. 1589. Ibid. fol. 261. b.

Letter to Archbifhop Laud from the Lords of the Council, requiring him to proceed with all Expedition in a Caufe depending before him, between the Inhabitants of Reculver and thofe of the Chapelries of St. Nicholas and Herne, touching the Repair

Repair of the Church and Steeple of Reculver. Dated from Whitehall the laſt Day of December, 1637. Reg. Laud, pars 1ma. fol. 286, a, b. (MSS. Lambeth.)
Archbiſhop Juxon augmented the Vicarage of Reculvere with 20l. per ann. By Indentures made 6 Mar. 13 Car. II. and one 25 Sept. 27 Car. II. (L. L.)
Pro reparatione ecclefiæ ibid. Vide HOTHE.

RIPPELE, Rect.
Compoſitio inter Abbat. S^{ti}. Auguſtini Cantuar. et Rectorem de Rippele, A. D. 1287. (printed in X. Script. col. 1942.)

ROLVYNDEN, Vic.
Commiſſio d'ni Will. Courtney Cant. Archiepiſc. directa mag. Tho. de Bakton Decan. de Arcubus, Ade de Mottrum Cancellario Archiepiſcopi

et Roberto Bradgare, Rect. Eccl. de Holynborne, ad inquirend. fuper fufficienti dotatione vicar. Eccl. parochial. de Rolvynden. Dat. apud Lambeth, 18 die Sept. A. D. 1383. Reg. Courtney, f. 54. b. (MSS. Lambeth.)

Appropriatio dict. Eccl. Collegio de Cobham.—Reg. Warham, fol. 156. Exemplificatio dict. Appropriationis, Dat. 16 Nov. 1604. Reg. Whitgift, pars III. fol. 283. a.

OLD RUMNEY, Rect.

In Mr. Lewis's MS. at Lambeth, p. 142, is a Note of the Tithes, Profits, and Advantages, belonging to this Rectory, copied from a Paper left in 1662, by Dr. Meric Cafaubon, to the Vicar of Monkton in Tenet.

ROMENAL, hodie NEW RUMNEY, Vic.

Ordinatio Vicar. Dat. 22 Octob. A. D.

A. D. 1402. Reg. Arundel. pars I. fol. 418. a. (MSS. Lambeth.)
Compofitio inter Rectores de Meddeley, al. Midley, et Veteri Romeney fuper decimis, et decretum Mag. Joh. Cooke, LL. D. Cancellar. domini Archiepifc. fuper eifdem. Dat. in Eccl. S^{ti}. Pauli, London. 15 die Feb. A. D. 1547. Reg. Cranmer, fol. 414. a. ad fol. 416. a. (MSS. Lambeth.)
Compofitio Vicár. de Romenal, et Affignatio portionis Vicar. per Thomam Archiepifc. Cant. apud Lambeth, 28 die Octob. A. D. 1402. (Regift. R. fol. 53. a.) MSS. Cantuar.
Ratificatio Prioris et Capit. Cant. fuper predictis, 10 die Decem. A. D. fupradicto. (Ibid. fol. 53. b.)
Chartæ Marifcorum de Romene, A. D. 1287, cum Ordinationibus, &c.

&c. ad eos spectant. Bibl. Cotton. Cleopatra. C. vii.—16.

SALTWODE, olim Vic. nunc Rect. cum capella de HYTHE.

Ordinatio Vicariæ. Dat. 17 Kal. Decemb. A. D. 1280. Reg. Peckham, fol. 171. b. (MSS. Lambeth.) —Alia Ordinatio (sans Date) sed inter 1206 et 1229. Chart. Miscellan. Vol. XI. N° 41. et N° 42. (MSS. Lambeth.)

SANDWICH, ST. CLEMENT, Vic.

The Church is of the Patronage of the Archdeacons of Canterbury. By an Agreement made between Abp. Whitgift, the Archdeacon, and Sir Roger Manwood the Archdeacon's Lessee, the Vicar had given him the Tenths of Corn and Hay within the said Parish, which before were due to the Archdeacon of Canterbury, and leased out by him, the Vicar

CANTERBURY. 101

Vicar paying Yearly to the said Archdeacon 7l. 6s. 8d. at the four usual times of Payment, by way of Composition for the Fine paid at Renewal. (MS. Lewis, p. 75.)

SANDWICH, B. MARIÆ, Vic.
Pro decimis de Pottakesdowne, vide EASTRY.

SELLYNG, Vic.
Ordinatio Vicar. A. D. 1349. (printed in X. Script. col. 2096.) Inquisitio de 110 garbis bladi pertinentibus ad Eccl. de Sellyng facta, A. D. 1274, et temp. Will. de Wylmenton tunc Camerarii Sti. Augustini Cantuar. Red Book of Canterbury, MS. in the Cotton Library (now in the British Museum) marked Claudius D. X. fol. 314. a. b. See also X. Script. col. 1922.

SESALTER, Vic. et HERNHILL, Vic.
Examinatio testis quoad limites parochiarum

rochiarum de Seafalter et Hernhill, 18 Junii, A. D. 1481. (Chartæ Ant. S. 415.) Archiv. Cantuar.

Examinatio alior. teftium fuper eadem materia, per Johannem Parmenter, in legibus Licentiat. Commiffar. Archiepifc. Cant. General. 23 Junii, A. D. fupradicto. (Chartæ Antiq. S. 414.) Ibid.

Prefentatio Tho. de Foxele ad Vicar de Scfaltre—falva Prior. et Convent. Cantuar. 3 folid. Cantuar. folvend. Reg. Henrici Prioris Cant. MS. in the Public Library at Cambridge, marked Ee. v. fol. 32. Terrier of Lands belonging to the Manor and Parfonage of Seafalter, A. D. 1621. Chartæ Mifcellaneæ, Vol. xi. N° 90. (MSS. Lambeth.)

SHELDWICK, Vic.

On the Diffolution of the Abby of St. Auftin, king Henry VIII. granted ed this Church and the Advowſon to the Dean and Chapter of Canterbury, by whom is paid to the Vicar of this poor Vicarage, a Stipend of 5l. per Ann. (MS. Lewis, p. 156.)

SHEPERSDWELL, al. SYBERTESWEALDE, Vic. olim Rect. See COLREDE.

Sententia judicum Delegatorum ſuper decimis de Sibertefwealde. Dat. menſe Julii, A. D. 1238. Leiger Book of the Priory of St. Martin at Dover, fol. 178. b. (MSS. Lambeth.)

Compoſitio inter Rect. de Sybertſwealde, et Prior. et Convent. S^{ti}. Martini de Dovorr. ſuper decimis. Ibid. Dat. ut ſupra. Ibid. fol. 179. a. Confirmatio Beati Edmundi Cant. Archiepiſc. ſuper ſententia lata de decimis de Sybertefwealde. Dat. ut ſupra. Ibid. fol. 179. b.

Compofitio inter Abbat. et Convent. S^{tæ}. Radegundis juxta Dovorr. et Prior. et Convent. S^{ti}. Martini de Dovorr. fuper decimis de Sybertefwealde. Dat. 6 Id. April. A. D. 1298. Ibid. fol. 180. a.

Augmented 20l. per ann. by Archbifhop Juxon. By Indentures, dat. 19 Jan. 12 Car. II. and another, dated 10 Apr. 28 Car. II. (L. L.)

SMALLHITHE, Capella.

Ordinatio domini Will. (Warham) Cant. Archiepifc. pro Capellano celebraturo in capella de Smallhithe, infra paroch. de Tenterden. Dat. apud Lambeth, 5 die Maii, A. D. 1509. Reg. Warham, fol. 338. b. 339. a. (MSS. Lambeth.)

The Capellane is chofen by the Inhabitants, and hath 50l. per ann. (MS. Lewis, p. 160.)

CANTERBURY.

SNARGATE. See COLREDE.

SNAVES, Rect.

Compofitio inter Abbat. et Convent. Sti. Auguftini Cant. et Henricum Rector de Snaves occafione fructuum et proventuum Eccl. de Snaves. Dat. Id. Feb. A. D. 1268. (printed in X. Script. col. 2113.)

STALESFIELD, Vic.

Augmented 25l. per ann. out of the Great Tithes, by Abp. Juxon. By Indentures, dated 11 July, 13 Car. II. and another, dated 17 April, 28 Car. II. (L. L.)

STANFORD CHAPEL. See OSTENHANGER.

STAPLEHERST, Rect.

Articles of Agreement concerning Tithes, between Robert Newman, Clerk, D. D. Rector of Stapleherft, and his Parifhioners. Dat. 23 Nov. 1604.

1604. Reg. Bancroft, fol. 125. a. (MSS. Lambeth.)
A further Order by Abp. Abbott, concerning the said Tithes, dated 7 Nov. 1611. Chartæ Miscellaneæ, vol. xi. N° 76. (MSS. Lambeth.)

STODMERSH, a Donative.
The Grant of Stodmersh Church to the Hospital of poor Priests in Canterbury, is printed in Somner's Antiq. of Cant. Appendix, p. 18.

STOKEBURY, Vic. See NEWINGTON.

STONE Chapel, to TENHAM.
The Great and Small Tithes are leased out by the Archdeacon of Canterbury, to whom they were appropriated. The Chapel long since demolished; but Elverton Manour pays no Tithes, they being granted by Langton, Archdeacon, to Christ Church, Canterbury (MS. Lewis, p. 175.)

STONE

CANTERBURY. 107

Stone in Oxene, Vic.

Ordinatio Vicariæ. Dat. apud Caſtrum de Saltwode, 2 Kal. Maii, A. D. 1360. Reg. Iſlip, fol. 159. a.—Exemplificatio Ordinationis prædict. Reg. Whitgift, pars 3ª. fol. 124. a. (MSS. Lambeth.)—Another, Dat. 5 Kal. Aug. A. D. 1360, is printed in X. Script. col. 2089, et 2122.

Ordinatio Vicariæ per Simonem Archiepiſc. Cant. (ſans Date.) Regiſter of St. Auſtin, Cant. called the Blacke Boke, MS. in the Cotton Library (now in the Britiſh Muſeum) marked Fauſtina A. 1. fol. 233. b.

Bond of Arbitration for referring certain Diſputes concerning the manner of paying of Vicarial Tithes in the Pariſh of Stone in the Iſle of Oxney, between Culpeper Savage, Vicar there, and the Pariſhioners of ſaid Pariſh, to the Determination

of

of Sir Walter Roberts, Bart. Sir Philip Boteler, Bart. and John Toke, Efq; with the Award of the faid Sir Walter Roberts and Sir Philip Boteler, 20 Jan. A. D. 1736. (Chartæ Ant. S. 404, 405.) Archiv. Cantuar.

STURMOUTH, Rect. See RECULVER. Indentura inter Dominum Will. (Courtney) Cant. Archiep'um ex parte una, et Will. (de Bottlefham) Roffen. Ep'um et Prior. et Capit. Eccl. Roffen. ex parte altera, concernent. Excambium fact. inter dict. Ep'um ac Prior. et Capit. ejufdem, de Jure Patronatus Ecclefiar. de Boxle et Sturmouth. Dat. apud Croydon, 1 die menfis Maii, A. D. 1391. Reg. Morton, Dene, Bourchier et Courtney, fol. 188. b. (MSS. Lambeth.)

CANTERBURY. 109

STURREYE, Vic.

Ordinatio Vicariæ. Dat. Id. Feb. A. D. 1323. Reg. Reynolds, fol. 103. a. (MSS. Lambeth) printed in X. Script. col. 2103.

Ordinatio Vicariæ per Walter. (Reynolds) Cant. Archiepif. (fans Date.) Regifter of St. Auftin, Cant. called the Blacke Boke, MS. in the Cotton Library (now in the Britifh Mufeum) marked Fauftina A. 1. fol. 234. b. 235. a.

SWINCKFIELD, Donative.

Now a Lay fee; being part of the Eftate of Sir Thomas Palmer, who allows 20l. per ann. to one in Holy Orders, to perform the parochial Duties, or ferve the Cure. (MS. Lewis, p. 181.)

TANTERDEN, Vic. See SMALLHITHE.

Taxatio five Ordinatio Vicar. de Tanterden, A. D. 1349. (printed

DIOCESE OF

in X. Script. col. 2100. Terrier of the Glebe of Tenterden, 19 Eliz. Chartæ Mifcellaneæ, Vol. xi. Nº 91. (MSS. Lambeth.)

TENHAM, Vic.

Augmented 10l. per ann. by Leafe, dated 10 Feb. 1672, between Sam. Parker, D. D. Archdeacon of Canterbury, and Sir Will. Hugeffen, of Linkfted, Co. Kent, Knt. (Cantuar.)

THANINGTON, Curacy.

Augmented by Abp. Juxon, out of the Great Tithes. By Indentures, dated 11 July, 13 Car. II. and 17 April, 28 Car. II. (L. L.)

THORNEHAM, Vic.

Compofitio five Concordia quoad Capell. de Aldington, facta inter Hen. Brockhill de Thorneham, in Com. Kantie, Arm. et Will. Merrick, Cleric. Vicar de Thorneham. Dat.

CANTERBURY.

24 die Aug. A. D. 1583. Reg. Grindall, fol. 577. b. 578. a. (MSS. Lambeth.)
Confirmatio, ratificatio, et approbatio, compofitionis five concordie prediɑ. faɑ. per Mag. Will. Awbrey, LL. D. Diœc. et Provinc. Cantuar. (fede Archiepifc. Cant. vacante) Cuftodem five Gardianum, et loci illius pro tempore Ordinarium. Dat. 26 die Aug. A. D. 1583. Ibid. fol. 578. a.

THRULEGH, al. THROWLEY, Vic.
Ordinatio Vicar. de Thrulegh, cum Capella de Wybrynton. Dat. 10 Kal. Sept. A. D. 1367. Reg. Langham, fol. 57. a, b. (MSS. Lambeth.) This parfonage was granted to the Prebend of Rugmere, in St. Paul's Cathedral, by a private Aɑ of Parliament, 32 Hen. VIII.

TIL-

TILMENSTON, Vic.

Carta Stephani (Langton) Cant. Archiepifc. concedens Fratribus Hofpitalis Hierofolimitani in Anglia Eccl. de Tilmanfton in proprios ufus habendam, refervatâ fibi et fuccefforibus Vicarii nominatione et inftitutione. — Vicarius habebit totum alteragium, et medietatem omnium decimarum ad eandem Ecclefiam pertinentium, et quoddam meffuagium, &c. (Liber de rebus ad Archidiaconatum Cantuar. fpectantibus, Liber Niger dictus, penes Archidiaconum Cant. in 8vo, fol. 42. MS. Wharton, p. 97. N° 582. (MSS. Lambeth.)
An ancient Copy of this Inftrument may be found in the Chartæ Mifcelleanæ, Vol. xi. N° 74 in the MS. Library at Lambeth.

Peti-

CANTERBURY.

Petition of Nicholas Carter, Vicar of Tilmanston, to Archbishop Wake, desiring Leave to take down the old Vicarage House and to erect a new one.—The Archbishop's Commission to Robert Lightfoot Rector of Deal, Edward Lloydd Rector of Ripple, and others, to view the Premisses and make a Report. Dat. June 8, 1719.—The Archbishop's Licence agreeable to the Petition, dated June 13, 1719. Reg. Wake, part 1. fol. 378. a, b. 379. a, b. 380. a. (MSS. Lambeth.)

TONGE, Vic.

Litera Cant. Archiep'i ad inquirend. super appropriatione facienda de Eccl. de Tonge. Dat. in Monaster. S. Radegund. 4 Id. Sept. A. D. 1325. Reg. Reynolds, fol. 138. b. Appropriatio dict. Eccl. Monaster. de Langedon. Dat. apud Lameth. 3 Id. Dec.

Dec. A. D. 1325. Ibid. fol. 143. a. 144. b. (MSS. Lambeth.)

Augmented 10l. per Ann. by Archbishop Juxon. By Indentures, dated 23 April, 14 Car. II. and another, 25 Jan. 24 Car. II. and another, dated 17 April, 28 Car. II. (L. L.)

TUNSTALL *, Rect.

Licentia domini Cant. Archiepisc. concessa Rob. Dixon, Rectori Eccl. paroch. de Tunstall, demoliend. vetus ruinosum ædificium vocat. *the Outhouse*, ad domum mansionalem Rectoriæ de Tunstall prædict. spectant. Dat. 20 die Aug. A. D. 1703. Reg. Tenison, pars 1ma. fol. 148. b. 149. a. (MSS. Lambeth.)

UPPECHIRCHE, Vic.

Commissio domini Archiepiscopi pro

---

* " The History and Antiquities of Tunstall in " Kent, by the late Edward Rowe Mores, F. A. S." form the first Number of the Bibliotheca Topographica Britannica, 1780, 4to.

augmentatione portionis Vicarii perpetui de Uppechirche, Abbati et Convent. de Infula Dei in Normannia, olim appropriat. ad v. marc. pro fuftentatione Vicar. perpet. ibid. Dat. Lambeth. 3 Non. Feb. A. D. 1369. Reg. Witlefeye, fol. 21. b. (MSS. Lambeth.)

WALDERSHARE, Vic.
Ratificatio fuper appropriatione dict. Eccl. Monafterio de Langedon. Dat. apud Lambeth. 12 Kal. April, A. D. 1322. Reg. Reynolds, fol. 138. a. (MSS. Lambeth.)
Augmented by Archbifhop Juxon 20l. per ann. By Indentures, dat. 15 Jan. 14 Car. II. and another, 8 Aug. 23 Car. II. (L. L.)

WALMERE, Vic.
Augmented by Archbifhop Juxon 20l. per ann. By Indentures, dated 15 Jan. 12 Car. II. another, dated

11 July, 13 Car. II. another dated 17 April, 28 Car. II. and another, dated 20 Nov. 28 Car. II. (L. L.)

WALTHAM et PETHAM, Vic.

Compofitio fuper Decimis Vicar. de Waltham. Dat. 10 Kal. April, A. D. 1276. Reg. Vet. Cart. Eccl. Chrifti Cant. In Bifhop Moore's Library at Cambridge.

Unio Ecclefiarum de Waltham et Petham. Dat. apud Lambeth, 4 die Julii 1698.—Confenfus domini Gulielmi Honywood, Baronet. patroni Vicar. de Petham ad unionem prædict. Dat. 4 die Julii, 1698. Reg. Tenifon, pars 1ma. fol. 116. a, b. (MSS. Lambeth.)

The Impropriation is charged with Forty Shillings a year to be paid as an Augmentation to the Vicar of Petham. (MS. Lewis, p. 127.)

WAREHORNE, Rect.

Concerning a Modus of one Shilling for every acre of marsh-land. See the Case of Ric. Bate, Rector, v. Sir Charles Sedley and others, in the Exchequer, 1726. In Vezey's Reports, Vol. II. Case 175.

Concerning a Modus for Hay and Small Tithes. See the Case of Bate, v. Hodges (in the Exchequer, 1722.), in Bunbury's Reports, 196.

Compositio super Decimis inter Prior. et Convent. de Horton et Hamonem Rect. de Warehorne per Sententiam Delegator. Papæ Innocentii III. Dat. in Eccl. Christi Cant. 7 Julii, 1220. (Reg. Priorat. de Horton. fol. 145 to 148.)

WESTBERE, Rect.

Compositio inter Priorem S. Gregorii Cant. et Rectorem de Westbere super quadam quantitate avenæ ac rebus aliis,

aliis. Dat. Lateran. 8 Kal. Mart. anno pontificatus Papæ Innocentii III. secundo. Honorius Rector solvet tres summas avenæ secundum mensuram qua mensuratur frumentum in civitate London. solvendas apud Risseburn integre scilicet ad natale Domini; salvo rectori Eccl. de Westbere omni jure parochiali in hominibus de Resseburn. Retent. Prior. et Convent. S. Gregorii solummodo decimas totius bladi omnium hominum predictor. de Risseburn, A. D. 1221. Chartæ et Concessiones factæ Canonicis S. Gregorii Cantuar. MS. in the Public Library at Cambridge, marked Ll. 11. 15.

WEST CLIVE, Vic.

Among the Archives of the Dean and Chapter of Canterbury is a Bull of Pope Boniface VIII. granting the said Church to the Monks there,

in

in proprios ufus, and granting an annual Penfion of Five Pounds Sterling for the Maintenance of the Vicar. The Bull is dated Avignon, 4 Kal. Sept. Anno Pont. 1°; that is, A. D. 1303.

WESTHETH, Vic.
Before the Civil War, here was paid to the Vicar 12 pence per acre of marfhland; but he who then had it, to ingratiate himfelf with the People, abated 2 pence an acre, fo it has been at 10 pence ever fince. (MS. Lewis, p. 199. b.)

WESTWELL, Vic.
Augmented by Archbifhop Juxon 30l. per ann. By Indentures, dated 23 April, 14 Car. II. and another, 20 Oct. 27 Car. II. (L. L.)
Archbifhop Tenifon gave in his life-time 50l. towards putting the Vicarage-houfe, which was gone pretty much

much to decay, into better repair, but it was laid out by his Grace's Truftee not fo much to the Advantage of the Houfe as it might have been. (MS. Lewis, p. 200.)

Dotatio Vicar. de Weftwell, per Henricum de Northewode, Rectorem dicte Eccl, die S^{ti}. Martini, A. D. 1298. (Chartæ Antiq. W. 185.) Archiv. Cantuar.

Literæ teftimoniales fuper affignatione portionis Vicar. de Weftwell, per Rectorem ejufdem ecclefiæ. Dat. fede Cant. vacante, per Henricum Priorem ecclefiæ Chrifti Cant. in octav. S^{ti}. Martini, A. D. 1293. (Reg. Berthona, part. 2. fol. 308. b.) MSS. Cantuar.

Compofitio inter mag. Joh. de la More, Rect. Eccl. de Weftwell et Steph. de Wilmington, Rect. de Bocton Alulphi, fuper decimis de
Hamelitis

CANTERBURY. 121

Hamelitis de Shotingdon, Chilberton, et Wike. Dat. apud Saltwood, 7 Id. Aug. 1305. fol. 39. a, b. of a MS. in the Lambeth Library, marked N° 244.

WHITSTAPLE, Vic.
Augmented by Archbifhop Juxon 10l. per ann. By Indentures, dated 14 March, 22 Car. II. and another 14 May, 22 Car. II. (L. L.)
Appropriatio ecclefiæ de Whitftaple, et affignatio ftipendii xii. marc. capellano dictæ ecclefiæ, per Thomam Archiepifc. Cant. apud Lambeth. fub anno ab incarnatione Domini 1477. die Febr. 10. (Regift. S. fol. 102, 103, 104, 105.) MSS. Cantuar.
Confirmatio Prioris et Capit. Cant. Dat. 27 die Martii, A. D. 1512. (Ibid. fol. 105. b.)

WING-

DIOCESE OF

WINGHAM, Cur.

Formerly a College. (See NONINGTON.)

WOODCHURCH, Rect.

Sententia d'ni Johannis (Peccham) Cant. Archiep'i fuper Decimis Eccl. parochial. de Wodechirche. Dat. apud Wyngham, 4 Kal. Oct. confecrat. noftre tertio (i. e. A. D. 1281.) Reg. Peccham, fol. 177. b. (MSS. Lambeth.)

WOODNESBORNE, Vic.

In the Deanry of Sandwich, was appropriated to the Abbey of Leedes, and on the Diffolution of that Abbey was granted by King Henry VIII. to the Dean and Chapter of Rochester, with the Patronage of it. The Church, dedicated to St. Mary, was of the Patronage of one Affelma, who gave this Church to the Prior and Convent of Leedes, and for that purpofe

CANTERBURY. 123

purpose surrendered it into the hands of Archbishop William (Corboyl) about A. D. 1122. who gave and granted it to the Canons, &c. in proprios usus perpetuo possidendam, specialiter ad inveniendum Canonicis, &c. necessaria indumenta. In 1267, a Dispute arose between the Prior and Convent of Ledes, Rectors of this Church, and Sir Adam Vicar, about the small Tithes, of the Crofts and Curtlages, in the Parish of Woodnesberghe, which was thus determined by the Prior of the Conventual Church of Rochester, the Pope's Delegate to judge in this Controversy, viz. that the said Prior and Convent, Rectors of the Church of Woodnesberghe, shall, quietly, for ever, wholly receive, without any exception, all the greater Tithes of Wheat, Barley, Oats, Beans,

Beans, Peafe, and of every fort of Blade, arifing or to arife, of all Lands, Crofts, Curtlages, &c. within the faid Parifh; and that the faid Prior and Convent fhall yearly pay for ever, to the faid Adam and his Succeffors, half a Seam of Barley, and half a Seam of Beans, at the Nativity of the Lord. In 1280 another Difpute was tried before the Archdeacon's Official, betwixt the Religious and Sir William, perpetual Vicar of this Church, about the payment of the Procuration of the Archdeacon of Canterbury, *cum in Ecclefia de Woodnefberghe memorata vifitaverit*, which was adjudged to be paid by the Vicar (MS. Lewis, p. 210.)

Compofitio de limit. parochial. inter Ecclefias de Eaftri et Woodnefburghe, viz. inter Prior. et Convent. Eccl.

Eccl. Chrifti Cant. ratione porcionis quam receperunt nomine benefici in Eccl. paroch. de Eaftri, &c. et Prior. et Convent. de Ledes, ratione Eccl. paroch. de Woodnefberghe, quam in proprios ufus tenent, A. D. 1302. Chartulary of Canterbury Cathedral Chart. 183.

WOTTON, Rect.
Augmented by Archbifhop Juxon 40l. per ann. Bifhop Kennet's Cafe of Impropriations, p. 256.

WYCHAM, Rect. et Vic. hodie Wickhambreux.
Unio et confolidatio Vicar. de Wycham ad Eccl. dicti loci. Dat. 7 Kal. April. A. D. 1322. Reg. Reynolds, fol. 102. b. (MSS. Lambeth.)
Compofitio inter Prior. et Convent. de Thunebrigg et Rad. Rector. Eccl. de Wycham fuper Decimis, A. D. 1238.

1238. (In the Chapter Houſe at Weſtminſter.)

Wye, Capella et Schola.

Charta Regis Henrici VIII. concedens Waltero Butler, Armig. Secretario Katherinæ Reginæ Angliæ, quaſdam Rectorias nuper Collegio de Wye modo diſſolut. ſpectantes, ſalvo ſalario 13 lib. 6 ſolid. et 8 den. ſolvend. ludimagiſtro, et ſtipend. 17 lib. ſolvend. duobus Capellanis apud Wye, a dicto W. Butler inveniendis. Dat. 15 die Martii, anno regni ſui 36°. (Chartæ Antiq. R. 25. Archiv. Cant.) Alſo at the Rolls Chapel, 20 pars Pat. 36 Hen. VIII.

Afterwards, anno 2 Car. I. another Grant of Wye, &c. was made to Robert Maxwell, Eſq. (in Purſuance of a Commiſſion iſſued under the Great Seal, to enquire into the Violations,

CANTERBURY.

lations, Omiffions, and Defaults, committed by Walter Butler and his Heirs, againſt the ſaid Letters Patent of 36 Hen. VIII. and alſo of an Inquiſition taken at Eaſt Greenwic, 3 die Oct. anno 20 Jac.) Proviſo that the ſaid Rob. Maxwell and his Heirs ſhall pay yearly to the Schoolmaſter of Wye ſixteen Pounds Sterling; and that he ſhall find one Chaplain to officiate at Wye, and pay him yearly Fifty Pounds Sterling for his Salary. T. R. 19 die Jan. See Sexta pars Paten. de anno regni Regis Caroli Secundi. See alſo Decima nona pars Paten. de anno Regis Caroli quinto. (In the Rolls Chapel.)

WYVELESBERGH, Vic.

Ordinatio Vicariæ. Dat. 5 Kal. Junii, A. D. 1356. Reg. Iſlip. fol. 119. a, b. (MSS. Lambeth.)

Dr. ——— Carter, by his laſt Will, gave the Leaſe which he had of the Parſonage of this Pariſh, from the Dean and Chapter of Canterbury, to the Vicar of this Place; the accuſtomed Fine for renewing this Leaſe every Seven Years being 21l. The Vicar pays 3l. per ann. to the Receiver of the ſaid Church, to be lodged in Bank, in order to the aboveſaid Renewal. (MS. Lewis, p. 204.)

Ordinatio Vicariæ. Dat. 5 Kal. Aug. A. D. 1360. (printed in X. Script. col. 2090. 2120. et 2122.

Ordinatio Vicariæ per Simonem (Mepeham) Cant. Archiepiſc. Dat. apud le Ford, 5 Kal. Oct. pont. ſui VII. (i. e. A. D. 1333.) Regiſter of St. Auſtin Cant. called the Blacke Boke, MS. in the Cotton Library (now in the Britiſh Muſeum) marked Fauſtina A. 1. fol. 127. a, b.

ADDENDA

TO THE

Diocese of CANTERBURY.

Aldington, Rect.
Of this Church the great Erasmus was Rector, by the Importunity of his Patron Archbp. Warham.
He was collated to it March 22, 1511; but he soon resigned it, on condition of a Pension of 20l. a year being paid to him out of it by Dr. *John Thornton*, the Archbishop's Suffragan; but there being a Misunderstanding betwixt him and *Erasmus* about paying this Pension,

and *Thornton* being besides taken up with a multiplicity of Business in doing his Suffragan's Office, the Archbishop collated *Richard Masters,* A. M. Nov. 18, 1514, of whom *Erasmus* gives this Character; " that " he was a young Man, well skilled " in Divinity." He was hanged with the others concerned with that Impostor *Elizabeth Barton*, a Servant Maid of this Parish, commonly called *The Holy Maid* of Kent. (MS. Lewis, p. 5.)

BIDDENDEN, Rect.
Here is a Free-school, founded by one of the Family of Mayney of this place, A. D. 1522, endowed with a House, and 20l. per ann. in the Gift of Feoffees.

A Farm called by the name of The Bread and Cheese Farm, rented at about

ADDENDA.

about 18l. per ann. *, and from its being given for a Free-gift of Bread and Cheese, to be given on every Easter-day, which is thus bestowed; viz. To all the poorest Sort a Three-penny Loaf of Bread and Nuncheen of Cheese; and to the richer, a little Manchet and Bit of Cheese; the Remainder to be distributed in money to the Poor. Given by two Persons, Women, who were Twins, and joined together in their bodies, who are said to have lived together 'till they were betwixt 20 and 30 Years old. The Estate in the Hands of Feoffees; and the Bread and Cheese is distributed by the Parish Officers to all that are at Church on Easter-day, after Divine Service. Ibid. p. 35.

* Six pounds at first.

ADDENDA.

GOODNESTONÈ, Donative.

Goodneftone Donative, or rather a perpetual Curacy, in the Deanery of Bridge.

This Church was appropriated to the Provoft and Canons of the Collegiate Church of Wingham, by whom was allowed to the Prieft who officiated here a yearly Penfion of 3 l. 6 s. 8 d. * above the Small Tithes.

On the Diffolution of the College, a Grant was made, &c. It is now Part of the Eftate of Sir Brooke Bridges, Bart. who is the Donor of this little Donative. Ibid. p. 114.

OSPRINGE, Vic.

Juft by the Way-fide was an Hofpital called Maifon Dieu, or Domus

* Now about 30 l. a Year.

Dei,

ADDENDA.

Dei, erected, as it is said, by Henry III.

It consisted of a Master, who was called Magister Hospitalis Beatæ Mariæ Virginis de Ospringe, three regular Freres, or Brethren *, whose Profession was of the Order of the Holy Cross, and of two Secular Clerks, whose Office it was to pray for the souls of Henry III. his Predecessors and Successors; and also to be hospitable, and give Entertainment to the King in his Progress this way, who had therefore an Apartment here called Camera Regis, and to the poor and needy Passengers and Pilgrims.

Here likewise the Knights Templars, and after them the Hospitallers, are said to have reposed themselves in

* Presbyteri Conversi.

their Progress towards their other Demesnes in this County.

After the Dissolution of the Alien Priories, the Parsonage of Ospringe was appropriated to this House, as was the Parsonage of Hedcrone; the other Part of their revenue lay at Lurenden, in Challock, and at Hokeling, Ryde, Marsh, and other places in the Isle of Shepway.

In the 22d Edw. IV. * the Master of this House or Hospital dying, and soon after one of the Brethren, the others suspected that it was the Plague of which they died, and accordingly all in great haste left the House, without so much as choosing another Master: By this means the Society was dissolved, and the Estate belonging to it escheated to the

* A D. 1482.

King, to whom it continued to belong till 10 Hen. VIII. when that Prince beftowed the Scite of this Houfe, and the Eftate belonging to it, on the Mafter and Fellows of St. John's College, in Cambridge. The Temporalities of this Houfe were valued in King Richard the Second's time at 5 1l. 5s. Ibid. p. 116.

A Memorial concerning the Fall of Ospringe Steeple, entered and fubfcribed at a Veftry, October 20, 1695.

The Steeple of Ofpringe was built of Flints, and very antient. The form was circular, like a round Tower; and by fome, thought to be a Danifh Building, and before the Conqueft. Over the Steeple was a tall Spire or Sharp, covered with Shingles of the height of fifty feet or more above the Flint-work; the Weight whereof did probably haften the Fall. It appears now that the whole Fabrick was all over decayed, rotten and ruinous, both in the Flint and Wood-work, and not likely to have held out much longer. But on Friday, being the eleventh Day of October, 1695, at which Time his Majefty William the Third, King of England, paffed by in his return from the Campaign in Flanders, the Bells were ordered to be rung for joy, to exprefs the Affections of this Neighbourhood to the King, &c. and fo continued to ring fome Hours after his Majefty paffed by; when about Three of the Clock in the Afternoon the whole Fabrick fell down, whilft they were in the act of ringing, without Damage to any Perfon, or to the Body of the Church, the Timber being generally all

ADDENDA. 137

all spoiled, but the Bells safe, only the Canons of the great Bell broke.

Edward Wamsley, } Churchwardens.
Edward Worrall,

Willam Mitchel, Overseer of the Poor.

Jonathan Bernard, Vicar.

John Knowler, Thomas Lake,
TheMarkofGeorge[C]Dinly. Ib.p.116.

One of the Cakes annually Given at Biddenden Church on Easter Sunday.

A LIST of the TERRIERS exhibited and remaining in the REGISTRY of the CONSISTORY COURT of CANTERBURY.

Parishes.	Dates.
Addisham, 2. one	November 11, 1615
another	No Date
Ash	No Date
Aldington	May 25, 1630
All Saints, Canterbury	No Date
Acris	May 21, 1630
St. Andrew, Canterbury	May 5, 1630
St. Alphage, Canterbury	1637
Alkham	May 6, 1630
Brookland	June 9, 1630
Boxley	May 22, 1630
Bilsington	No Date
Bredhurst	August 22, 1615,
Brenzett, 2. one	No Date
another	No Date

Birch-

LIST of TERRIERS, &c. 139

Parishes.	Dates.
Birchington	—— No Date
Bonnington	—— May 23, 1630
Beaksbourn	—— May 6, 1630
Buckland (by Faversham)	} May 7, 1630
Boughton under the Blean one	} 1634
another	— August 30, 1615
and another	— May 12, 1630
Bredhurst, 2. one	— May 10, 1630
another	— May 18, 1637
Bishopsbourne	—— May 6, 1630
Brabourn	—— No Date
Bennenden	—— April 30, 1630
St. Mary Bredman, Canterbury	} May 10, 1630
Barfrestone	—— May 10, 1630
Lapchild	—— May 2, 1630
Brook	—— April 28, 1630
St. Mary Bredin, Canterbury	} August 24, 1615
Boughton Monchelsea	April 27, 1630
Bobbing	—— April 23, 1630
Burmarsh	—— April 20, 1630
Challock, 2. one	— March 10, 1638
Chart next Sutton	— April 26, 1630
Chiflet	—— May 20, 1630
Coledred	—— May 9, 1630
Capel le Fern	—— May 3, 1630

Little

LIST of TERRIERS, &c.

Parishes.	Dates.
Little Chart	May 10, 1630
Cheriton	May 9, 1630
Great Chart	May 9, 1630
Chillenden	May 6, 1630
Challock, a second	November 10, 1615
Charing, 2. one	August 24, 1615
another	April 9, 1630
Chillham	{ No Date exhibited / April 9, 1630 }
Dimchurch	1630
Deal	May 6, 1630
Denton	April 27, 1630
Doddington	May 1, 1630
St. Dunstan, Canterbury	April 27, 1630
Debtling	October 13, 1615
East Langdon	No Date
Elham	No Date
Elmstone	No Date
Elmsted	April 28, 1630
Egerton	October 13, 1615
Eastry, 2. one	No Date
another	August 24, 1637
Ewell	April 27, 1630
Fordwich	May 12, 1630
Frinsted	April 30, 1630
Faversham	April 13, 1630
Fairfield	August 23, 1615
Frittenden	April 27, 1630

Gustone

LIST of TERRIERS, &c.

Parishes.	Dates.
Gustone	May 7, 1630
Goudherst	May 25, 1630
St. George, Canterbury	May 13, 1630
Graveney	May 7, 1630.
Goodneftone, by Faverfham	May 6, 1630,
Harrietfham	No Date
Little Hardres	May 25, 1630
Hawkinge	No Date
Hawkhurft	May 10, 1630
Hackington, alias St. Stephen's	May 16, 1630
Holy Crofs, Weftgate, Canterbury	May 13, 1630
Monks Horton	May 3, 1630
Halftow	May 3, 1630
Hartlip	May 10, 1630
Hope	May 3, 1630
Hougham	No Date, exhibited April 29, 1630
Hinxhill	April 20, 1630
Haftingleigh	April 28, 1630
Harbledown	April 28, 1630
Great Hardres	1630, exhibited May 1, 1630
Hearne	Auguft 28, 1615
Hollingbourne	Auguft 20, 1615
St. James's, Dover	1638

Ick-

Parishes.	Dates.
Ickham, 2. one	August 25, 1615
another	May 12, 1630
Iveychurch	May 9, 1630
Kingstone	May 3, 1630
Kennington	May 10, 1630
Kingsdown	April 26, 1630
Kingsnorth	No Date
Lydden	April 25, 1630
Littlebourne	April 29, 1630
Leysdown	May 17, 1637
St. Lawrence, Thanet	May 24, 1630
Linsted	May 16, 1630
Lyminge	May 10, 1630
Luddenham	No Date, exhibited May 12, 1630
Lympne	May 9, 1630
Lenham	April 30, 1630
Loose	May 5, 1630
Leaveland	May 2, 1630
Linton	April 26, 1630
Monkton, 2, one	July 7, 1630
another	July 17, 1682
St. Mary in the Marsh	June 7, 1630
Milsted	May 16, 1630
Midley	May 14, 1630
St. Martin, Canterbury	May 9, 1630
Mersham	May 1, 1630
Marden	May 3, 1630

Milton

LIST of TERRIERS, &c.

Parishes.	Dates.
Milton by Sittingbourne	May 8, 1630
Minster in Thanet	May 13, 1630
St. Mary Magdalen, Cant.	April 27, 1630
St. Nicholas at Wade	June 10, 1630
Newenden	May 7, 1630
New Church	May 26, 1630
Norton	May 7, 1630
Newington (by Hythe)	May 1, 1630
Newington (by Sittingbourne)	May 7, 1630
Nonnington	August 29, 1615
Northborne	May 7, 1630
Ospringe	May 22, 1630
Orlestone	May 16, 1630
Otham	May 24, 1630
Owre	May 3, 1630
Otterden	May 10, 1630
Preston (by Faversham)	September —, 1630
St. Peter, Thanet	May 22, 1630
Preston (by Wingham)	No Date
Postling	No Date
St. Peter, Canterbury	May 11, 1630
Patrixbourne	May 6, 1630
Petham	April 28, 1630

St.

LIST of TERRIERS, &c.

Parishes.	Dates.
St. Paul, Canterbury	April 28, 1630
Ringwould	— May 11, 1630
Rodmersham	— May 10, 1630
Ruckinge	⸻ May 1, 1630
River	⸻ April 28, 1630
Reculver	— October 1, 1630
Old Romney	— May 17, 1630
Ripple	⸻ May 6, 1630
New Romney, 3. one	No Date
another	July 7, 1634
another	August 29, 1615
Saltwood	— August 25, 1615
Standford	— August 23, 1615
Sandherst	— September 24, 1630
Sturry	— May 1, 1630
Staple, 2. one	— August 22, 1615
another	— May 28, 1630
Sittingbourne	— 1630
Stockberry	— May 20, 1630
Stowting	— May 16, 1630
Seasalter	— No Date
Sevington	— May 16, 1630
Stourmouth	— May 3, 1630
Stallesfield	— May 13, 1630
Snave	— May 4, 1630
Smarden	— May 2, 1630
Sheldwich	— May 9, 1630
Stapleherst	— May 10, 1630
Swackliff	— April 6, 1630

Sellinge

LIST of TERRIERS, &c.

Parishes.	Dates.
Sellinge	April 27, 1630
Smeeth, 2. one	August 27, 1615
another	May 10, 1630
Sheperdswell, alias Sibertswould	May 2, 1630
Sutton, by Dover	April 27, 1629
Tunstall	May 17, 1630
Tilmanston	Dated 1630, exhibited May 12, 1630
Tong	May 3, 1630
Upchurch	May 10, 1630
Westwell, 2. one	March 3, 1634
Warden	May 13, 1634
Warehorne	June 21, 1630
Willesborough	May 15, 1630
Woodnesborough	May 11, 1630
Whitstable	No Date, exhibited May 14, 1630
Walmer	April 29, 1630
Witchling	May 6, 1630
Whitfield, alias Beaufield	No Date, exhibited May 12, 1630
Waldershare	No Date, exhibited May 12, 1630
Wickhambreux	May 3, 1630
Womenswould,	May 1, 1630
Waltham	April 28, 1630
Westbeer	April 28, 1630

Parishes.	Dates.
West-Langdon	No Date, exhibited April 28, 1630
Westwell, another	August 23, 1615
Womenswould, another	September 2, 1615
Woodchurch, 2. one	August 23, 1615
another	May 15, 1637
Wootton, 2, one	May 10, 1630
another	May 2, 1675
Wittersham	October 25, 1615
St. Alphage, Canterbury	April 27, 1747
Adisham, with the Chaple of Staple	No Date exhibited May 14, 1744
Challock	April 16, 1745
Godmersham	April 15, 1745
Ickham	May 5, 1744
St. Nicholas at Wade	May 12, 1744
Nonnington and Womenswould	May 14, 1744
Reculver and Hoath	May 29, 1746
Sturry	May 29, 1746
Saltwood	August 26, 1750
Westwell	April 9, 1751
Woodchurch	Exhibited at the Commissary's Visitation April 27, 1747.

A

A LIST of the TERRIERS remaining in the REGISTRY of the ARCHDEACON of CANTERBURY.

Parishes.	Dates.
ST. Andrew, Canterbury, 2. one	May 21, 1634
the other	September 23, 1635
Appledore, 2. one	August 20, 1615
another	In the Year 1637
Acris	No Date
Ashford	September 2, 1615
Boxley, 2. one	August 18, 1615
another	In the Year 1637
St. Mary Bredin, Canterbury	September 24, 1615
Boughton Aluph	No Date, exhibited September 6, 1615
Boughton Malherb, 2. one	September 26, 1615
another	June 20, 1637
Bobbing, 2. one	August 20, 1615
another	May 19, 1637

Bersted;

148 LIST of TERRIERS, &c.

Parishes.	Dates.
Bersted, 2. one	— The Date not perfect
another	— September 22, 1634
Borden, 2. one	— August 26, 1615
another	— May 18, 1637
Bennenden	— October 1, 1615
Papchild	— September 4, 1615
Biddenden	— September 13, 1615
Boxley	{ May 18, in the 3d Year of Edward VI.
Brenfett	{ No Date, exhibited August 20, 1615
Barfreftone	— August 17, 1615
Bredgar	— August 21, 1615
Bicknor	— September 15, 1615
Bonnington	— August 21, 1615
Brookland	— August 27, 1615
Beauxfield	— October 16, 1615
Burmarsh	— August 28, 1615
Brabourn	— October 18, 1615
Buckland, by Faversham	} September 2, 1615
Bilsington	— September 20, 1615
Barham	— June 8, 1634
Bishopsbourn	— June 22, 1634
Brook	— August 18, 1615
Boughton Monchelsea	August 20, 1615
Chartham	— August 25, 1615
St. Cosmus Blean	-- August 25, 1615
Great Chart	— October 1, 1613
Crundal	— No Date

St.

LIST of TERRIERS, &c.

Parishes.	Dates.
St. Clement Sandwich	October 6, 1615
Charlton, 2. one	— November 5, 1615
another	— May 4, 1634
Coldred	———— September 22, 1615
Cranbrook, 3. one	— September 28, 1615
another	— April 20, 1634
and another	— May 22, 1637
Chillenden	———— September 30, 1615
Capel le Fern	——— October 18, 1615
Chiflet, 2. one	— August 17, 1615
another	— { No Date, exhibited / July 17, 1682
Cherriton, 2. one	— August 18, 1615
another	— May 4, 1637
Chart Sutton	——— August 24, 1615
Doddington	——— August 29, 1615
Denton	——— No Date
St. Dunstan, Canterbury	} October 27, 1615
Dimchurch	——— September 17, 1615
Elham	——— September 24, 1615
Eythorn	} No Date, exhibited / August 26, 1615
Ewell	——— August 26, 1615
Elmsted	——— August 23, 1615
Eastling,	——— September 18, 1615
Frinsted	——— August 19, 1615
Fordwich	——— August 21, 1615
Folkstone	— November 2, 1615

Parishes.	Dates.
Feversham	September 11, 1615
Goodneftone, by Feversham	August 20, 1615
Goudherft	September 17, 1615
St. George, Canterbury	September 18, 1615
Graveney	October 1, 1615
Little Hardres	September 30, 1615
Halden, 2. one	August 21, 1615
another	June 14, 1634
Hope	No Date
Harrietfham. 2. one	September 17, 1615
another	October 7, 1663
Hackington	September 11, 1615
Horton	September 4, 1615
Hartlip	August 21, 1615
Hawkinge	No Date
Hougham	No Date, exhibited September 21, 1615
Headcorn	August 18, 1615
Halftow	December 31, 1615
Hothfield	September 30, 1615
Hinxhill	No Date
Hawkhurft, 3. one	September 17, 1615
another	May 5, 1634
and another	May 13, 1637
Ham, 2. one	No Date
another	No Date, exhibited September 25, 1637

Hafting-

LIST of TERRIERS, &c.

Parishes.	Dates.
Haftingleigh	—— Auguft 18, 1615
St. John's, Thanet, 2. one	} In the Year 1615
another	—— In the Year 1637
Iwade, 2. one	—— Dated Auguft 1615
another	—— June 4, 1637
Kingftone	—— Auguft 22, 1615
Kingfnorth	—— No Date
Kenardington, 2. one	September 16, 1615
another	- June 29, 1637
Kingfdown	— Auguft 10, 1615
Lynton	—— No Date
Lydden	—— Auguft 18, 1615
Littlebourne	—— October 16, 1615
Weft Langdon	— Auguft 27, 1615
Lenham	—— September 12, 1615
Leaveland	—— September 12, 1615
Langley	—— September 13, 1615
Eaft Langdon, 2. one	No Date
another	- In the Year 1634
Linfted	{ No Date, exhibited / Auguft 31, 1615
Leyfdown	—— October 3, 1615
St. Lawrence, Thanet, 2. one	} No Date
another	{ No Date, exhibited / May 10, 1637
Lympne	—— September 4, 1615

St.

LIST of TERRIERS, &c,

Parishes.	Dates.
St. Mildred, Canterbury	September 20, 1615
Great Mongeham, 2. one	October 9, 1615
another	May 4, 1634
Marden	September 17, 1615
Milsted	August 22, 1615
St. Mary Magdalen, Canterbury	November 27, 1615
Little Mongeham	No Date, exhibited April 29, 1615
Minster, Thanet	No Date, exhibited September 11, 1615
St. Mary Sandwich	No Date
St. Mary in the Marsh	September 17, 1615
Molash	October 1, 1615
Milton, by Sittingbourne	September 2, 1615
Mersham	August 20, 1615
Minster in Sheppy	August 27, 1615
Murston	No Date
Norton	August 31, 1615
Newenden, 2. one	September 8, 1615
another	June 9, 1634
Nackington	No Date, exhibited August 27, 1615
Newington (by Sittingbourne)	August 10, 1615

New-

LIST of TERRIERS, &c.

Parishes.	Dates.
Newington (by Hythe)	September 26, 1615
Northborne	September 14, 1615
Newnham	August 29, 1615
Owre	No Date, exhibited August 29, 1615
Ospringe, one	September 18, 1615
another	In the Year 1637
and another	In the Year 1760
Orlestone	September 15, 1615
Otterden	September 26, 1615
St. Peter, Canterbury	August 16, 1615
St. Peter, Thanet, 2. one	October 8, 1615
another	May 22, 1637
Preston (by Faversham)	In the Year 1615
Postling	October 13, 1615
Pluckley	May 4, 1634
Ripple	August 7, 1615
Ringwould	October 1, 1615
River	August 18, 1615
Rodmersham	September 4, 1615
Rainham	August 18, 1615
Ruckinge	September 15, 1615
Old Romney	No Date
Sellinge	August 20, 1615
Selling	August 30, 1615
Snargate	No Date

154 LIST of TERRIERS, &c.

Parishes.	Dates.
Stalesfield	— August 23, 1615
Swackliff	— August 19, 1615
Stowting	— September 1, 1615
Sandherst, 2. one	— August 21, 1615
another	- June 9, 1634
Stelling	{ No Date, exhibited May 30, 1637
Sheldwich	— No Date
Sutton (by Dover)	August 20, 1615
Stone in Oxney	— April 17, 1634
Sevington	—— September 20, 1615
Sturry	——— August 19, 1615
Smarden, 2. one	— August 20, 1615
another	- May 22, 1637
Sholden	——— October 20, 1615
Shadoxherst	— September 26, 1615
Sittingbourne	— In the Year 1615
Sheperdswell	— October 15, 1615
Snave	— October 4, 1615
Stockberry, 2. one	-- August 21, 1615
another	-- May 8, 1637
Stodmarsh	——— August 21, 1615
Sutton Valence, 2. one	August 21, 1615
another	May 10, 1634
Throwleigh	— September 5, 1615
Tenterden, 3 one	- August 9, 1615
another	- June 13, 1634
and another	- December 1, 1637
Tilmanstone	— September 30, 1615

LIST of TERRIERS, &c.

Parishes.	Dates.
Thornham	August 21, 1615
Tong	August 22, 1615
Tenham	October 2, 1615
Tunstal	September 21, 1615
Ulcomb	June 19, 1637
Upchurch	August 20, 1615
Wotton	August 20, 1615
Wickhambreux, 2. one	} In the Year 1615
another	May 11, 1637
Woodnesborough, 2. one	} November 6, 1615
another	April 12, 1675
Witchling	September 21, 1615
Walmer	October 9, 1615
Wormshall	August 22, 1615
Willesborough	No Date
Waltham	September 24, 1605
Warden	August 24, 1615
Warehorn, 2. one	No Date
another	May 17, 1637
Westbeer	September 30, 1615
West Hythe	September 5, 1615

ENDOW-

ENDOWMENTS
OF
VICARAGES
IN THE
DIOCESE
OF
ROCHESTER.

ENDOWMENTS of VICARAGES

IN THE

DIOCESE of ROCHESTER.

AYLESFORD, Vic.
Ordinatio feu Compofitio Vicariæ Reg. Hamo de Hethe, fol. 32. Ordinatio Vicariæ. Dat. apud Trottefclive, 17 kal. Aug. A. D. 1293. Appropriatio dict. Eccl. Hofpital. B. M. de Strodes per G. Roffen. Epifc. (E. Regiftr. Eccl. Roffen.) Conceffio Prioris et Convent. Roffen. fuper appropriatione Eccl. de Aylefford. ibid. Confirmatio Huberti Cant. Archiepi. fuper appropriatione predict. ibid. Confirmatio Ricardi Regis fuper appropriatione predict. ibid. Printed in Mr. Thorpe's *Regiftrum*

gistrum Roffense, p. 149. 152. 153. which is hereafter called R. R.

AYNESFORD, Vic. (Peculiar Cant.) See EYNESFORD and FRENYNGHAM. By Indenture Tripartite, dat. 14 Nov. 33 Car. II. between Francis Porter, Rector of the Parish Church of Aynesford, in the County of Kent, of the First Part; George Gifford, of Pennis, in the Parish of Fawkesham, in the said County of Kent, Esq. of the Second Part; and Edward Tilson, Vicar of Eynsford aforesaid, of the Third Part. A yearly Rent of 20l. is reserved to the Vicar of Aynesford and his Successors out of the Rectory. (Lambeth Leases.) Confirmed A.D. 1667; also confirmed 25 June, 1707, in Pursuance of the Queen's Letter to the Bishops, Deans, &c. for the Augmentation of Vicarages See the

ROCHESTER. 161
the Archbishop of Canterbury's Entry Book, vol: II. p 112.
BARMING, alias BARMINGE, Rect. Concessio Annuæ pensionis duorum Solidorum de Eccl. de Barmling Priori et Convent. de Ledis per G. Roffen. Episc. (sans date) E. Reg. Eccl. Roffen. Decretum super Unione Ecclesiarum de Barming et Nittlestede. Dat. in Eccl. de Nittlestede, 24 April, A. D. 1408. Autog. penes Dec. et Capit. Roffen. (printed in R. R. p. 161, 162.)

BEXLEY (Peculiar Cant.) Vic. Assignatio porcionis Vicarii de Bexle (sans date) sed tempore Stephani Langton, Cant. Archiep'i, i. e. inter A. D. 1216 et A. D. 1229. Reg. Warham, f. 151. (MSS. Lambeth.) Ordinatio Vicariæ de Byxhill, per S. (i. e. Stephanum Langeton) Cant. Archiep'um; olim appropriat. Prior.

M et

et Convent. Sti Trinitatis London. per W. (i. e. Will. Corboyl) Cant. Archiep'um. Hiis Teftibus Mag. Simone de Langeton fratre noftro, Mag. Will. de Barden, Mag. Tho. de Frefcham, Rob. de Briftoll, Mag. Adde Tilnea, Mag. Walter de Hemefham, Mag. Joh. Phyfico, Will. de Bofco, Joh. de Waltham, Vincentio de Norwico, et multis aliis. In part of an original Regifter Book of the Priors of the Trinity, London, formerly A. D. 1767. in the Library of James Weft, Efq. (in Lord Shelburne's Library, 1781.) Interlocutaria fententia Mag. Reynerii de Viterbio Auditoris Papæ fuper decimis dict. Eccl. Dat. 13 Jan. A. D. 1255 Taxatio Vicariæ per (S. Langton) Cant. Archiep'um, et 23 Chart. Antiq. ad dict. Eccl. fpectant. extant hodie (1781) in the Chapter Houfe at Weftminfter.

BIR-

Birling, Vic.

Decretum Johannis (Stafford) Cant. Archiep'i fuper Augmentatione porcionis Vicar. de Birling. Dat. in Eccl. de Lamehithe, 20 die Maii, A. D. 1447. Archiv. Eccl. Cathedral. Roffen. Printed in R. R. p. 171. et feq. Proceedings upon the Augmentation of this Vicarage, Act. Cur. Confift. Roffen. 1436. 1443. fol. 193. a. 194. a. 195. a. 230. a. 234. a. 242. b. 248. b. 257. b.

Bradstede, Rect. (Peculiar Cant.)

Inquifitio facta de Terris Glebal. fubftract. per Parochianos de Bradftede et fententia Simonis (Iflip) Cant. Archiep'i de Gleba Eccl. predict. Dat. apud Maghfield, 10 kal. Julii, A. D. 1352. Reg. Iflip. fol. 57. b. (MSS. Lambeth.)

Brenchley, Vic.

The Rectory was impropriated to

Cardinal College, Oxon. See Strype's Eccl. Memor. vol. I. N° 28. Appendix.

Appropriatio dict. Eccl. Monaster. de Thonebregge, et Ordinatio Vicariæ, per H. Roffen. Ep'um. Orig. penes Dec. et Capit. Roffen. (Printed in R. R. p. 185.)

BURHAM, Vic.

The particular Endowment and Onera of this Vicarage are in Regiftr. E. Lowe. f. 204. b. Ordinatio Vicariæ. Dat. apud Burgham, 4 kal. Dec. A. D. 1302. Reg. Will. de Bottlesham, f. 126. b. Inquifitio et Dotatio Vicariæ. Dat. 4 Nov. 1445. ibid. fol.

Ordinatio Vicariæ. Dat. 4 kal. Dec. A. D. 1302. Reg. Priorat. Hofpit. S. Joh. Bibl. Cotton. Nero E. VI. (Printed in R. R. p. 196.)

On

ROCHESTER. 165

On the 26 April, 1567, the Crown granted a Leafe of the Rectory and Tithes of Burgham to Doctor ... * Cefar for 21 Years, paying annually to the Vicar of Burgham two Quarters of Corn. (Particulars of Leafes in the Augmentation Office, Kent, Roll V. N° XXII.)

CHALKE, Vic.
Ordinatio Vicariæ. A. D. 1327. Reg. Hamo de Hethe, f. 3.
Alia Ordinatio. Dat. apud Hallynge, 24 die Maii, 1391. Reg. J. de Bottleſham, f. 14. a. (Printed in R. R. p. 205.)

CHATHAM. See ROCHESTER CHURCHES.
CHESLEFEILD, Rect.
Decretum Johannis Roffen. Ep'i de annua penſione ſolvend. Rectoii de Chefleſeild de quodam Campo in

* Sic Orig.

Farne-

Farneborough. Reg. Spir. Eccl. Roffen. (Printed in R. R. p. 354. et seq.)

CHEVENING, Rect.

A Commiffion for Exchange of Lands in this Parifh between the Earl of Stanhope and Edward Gee, D. D. Rect. of Chevening. Dat. 14 June, 1718. Reg. Wake. Vol. I. fol. 376. a. (MSS. Lambeth.)

CHIDINGSTON, Rect.

Archbifhop Wake's Licence to Tho. Jenifon, the Rector, to take down fome ufelefs Buildings belonging to the Parfonage Houfe, A. D. 1728, 14 Sept. Reg. Wake, vol. II. p. 325.

Another Licence to the faid Rector to make fome Alterations in the Parfonage Houfe, dated 6 Aug. 1733 ib. fol. 328. a. b. (MSS. Lambeth.)

CLYVE,

ROCHESTER.

CLYVE, al. CLIFFE, at Hoo (Peculiar. Cant. Rect.)

Compositio inter Prior. et Capit. Cant. et Mag. Ricardum Rectorem Eccl. de Clyve de Decimis Mariscorum ibid. Act. in Eccl. Parochial. de Boxele, mense Maii, anno Gratie 1229. Chartæ Antiquæ C. 230. Registratur in Libro C. f. 42. a. (penes Dec. et Capit. Cantuar.)

Charta indentata dictæ Compositionis. Chartæ Antiquæ. C. 231. (ibid)

Confirmatio Ricardi Archiep'i Cantuar. super eadem Compositione. Dat. ut supra. Reg. C. f. 43. a. (Ibid.)

Transcriptum Compositionis inter Priorem et Capit. Cant. et Mag. Ricardum quondam Rectorem Eccl. de Clive de Decimis. Item Transcriptum Confirmationis Ricardi Archiep'i Cant. Act. Anno Gratie 1229,

1229, mense Maii. Dat. sub sigillo Henrici Prioris S*t*. Gregorii in Crastino S*ti*. Barnabe Apostoli A. D. 1277, Chartæ Antiquæ. C. 4:7. Ibid.

Confirmatio Johannis Archiep'i Cant. Compositionis olim facte, et confirmate per Ricardum Archiep. Cant. Dat. A. D. 1229, inter Prior. et Capit. Cant et Mag. Ric. de Walingford, Rect. Eccl. de Clive. de Decimis Barcariorum de Clyve. Dat. apud Slyndone, 6 Id. Oct. A. D. 1291. Chartæ Antiquæ. C. 388. Regist. in Lib. C. f. 44. a. Ibid.

Charta Hugonis de Mortuomari Rectoris Eccl. de Clive de Decimis non petendis Berchariorum et Molendinorum Prioris et Capit. Cant. in Parochia de Clive ; ac Decimis Minoribus ex Manerio suo de Clive proventibus. Salvo jure successor. Dat. A. D. 1254. Die Dominica

ROCHESTER. 169

ante Feſtum beati. Martini hyemalis. Chartæ Antiquæ. C. 439. (Ibid.)

Compoſitio inter eoſdem et Mag. Richard de Stratford. Rect. Eccl. de Clyve ſuper eiſdem Decimis. Dat. London. A. D. 1277. Menſe Nov. Chartæ Antiquæ. B. 337. Regiſt. in Lib. E. f. 43. a. (Ibid.)

Compoſitio inter eoſdem et D'um Philippum de Wyleby Rector. Eccl. de Clyve dè eiſdem Decimis. Dat. London, Non. April. A. D. 1283. Chartæ Antiquæ. C. 237. Regiſtratur in Lib. C. fol. 43. a. (Ibid.)

Confirmatio Johannis Archiep'i Cant. ſuper eadem Reg. C. f. 43. b. (Ibid.)

Alia Charta de eadem Materia. Chartæ Antiquæ. C. 262. (Ibid.)

Acta in Cauſa Decimar. inter Priorem et Capit. Cant. et Johannem de Beſtane, Rector Eccl. de Clive, 10 Februarii,

Februarii, A. D. 1289. Chartæ Antiquæ. C. 219. (Ibid.)

Compofitio inter eofdem et eundem Mag. Joh'em de Beftane de decimis apud Clive. Dat. Cantuar. kal. Augufti, A. D. 1290. Reg. C. f. 44. a. (Ibid.)

Refignatio Mag. Joh'is de Beftan, Rectoris de Clive de Decimis Marifcor. de Clive. Dat. Kal. Augufti, A. D. 1290. Chartæ Antiquæ. C. fo. 90. 124. (Ibid).

Acta in Caufa Decimarum inter eofdem et Jacobum de Cobeham, Rect. Eccl. de Clive, 28 April, 1305. Chartæ Antiquæ. C. 124. (Ibid.)

COBHAM, Vic. See Shorne.

COWDHAM, Vic.

Appropriatio dict. Eccl. Prior. et Convent. Monafterii Monial de Kilbourne, per Thomam Roffen, Ep'um. Confirmatio ejufdem per Prior. et Capit.

ROCHESTER.

Capit. Roffen. Dat. apud Trottef-cliff, 27 Junii, A. D. 1377. Licentia Regia fuper appropriatione prædict. 1 Dec. anno 50. E. 3. Reg. J. Fifher, fol. 56. a.—Nomina Camporum Decime de Bettrede in Paroch. de Codham. (Printed in R. R. p. 264.)

CRAY, ST. MARY CHAPEL. See ORPINGTON.

CUXTON, al. COOKSTONE, Rect.
Conventio inter Rectorem de Cucleftane et Magiftrum Hofpital. B. M. de Strode fuper Decimis in Parochia de Cockelftane, A. D. 1277. Reg. Temp. Roffen. f. 22. a. Charta Rectoris de Cokelftane fuper Penfione annua 10 fol. conceffa Hofpitali de Strode folvenda de Eccl. de Cokeftane, A. D. 1295. (Printed in R. R p. 259, 260.)

DA-

DIOCESE OF

Darenth (Peculiar Cant.) Vic.
Ordinatio Vicariæ. Reg. Spirit. Roffen.
F. fol. 14. b. 83. b. 84. a.
Appropriatio dict. Eccl. facta Monachis Roffen. (fans date) in Archivis Dec. et Cap. Roffen. Augmentatio Vicariæ de Darenth. A. D. 1290. E. Reg. Spiritual Eccl. Roffen. Ordinatio Johannis Cant. Archiep'i super portionibus Eccl. de Darente, Dat. apud Mortlake, 3 Die Dec. A. D. 1292. E. Reg. Eccl. Roffen. Articles of Agreement about Lands, Tenements, &c. within this Parish, between the Prior and Convent of Rochester and John Crepehegge, dated 12 Feb. 20 E. IV. Compofitio inter Vicarium de Darente et Inhabitantes infra precinctum Capelle de Helles. Dat. apud Oteford. ult. die Jan. A. D. 1522. Printed in R. R. p. 272. to p. 278. This last

last Composition is also extant in Reg. Warham, fol. 317. a. b. (MSS. Lambeth.)

DARTEFORD, Vic.

Ordinatio Laurent. Roffen. Ep'i super pensione decem marcarum solvend. Prior. et Convent. Roffen. per Vicarium de Darteford. Dat. 10 kal. Aug. A. D. 1299. Autog. penes Dec. et Cap. Roffen.—Ordinatio Walteri Cant. Archiep'i super eadem. Dat. apud Lamhethe, 19 kal. Sept. A. D. 1300. Certificatio Sententiæ Diffinitive in Causa inter Vicarium de Darteford et Ep'um Roffen. super Pensione decem Marcarum per Inspeximus. Dat. Cant. 7 kal. Julii, A.D.1313. Sententia super Decimis. Dat. 4 kal. Aug. A. D. 1315. Autog. penes Dec. et Cap. Roffen. Certificatorium Executionis Mandati Officialis Cant. super Pensione decem

decem marcarum debit. Priori et Conv. Roffen. et proveniente de Vicaria de Darteford. Dat. apud Stone, 16 kal. April, A. D. 1323. E. Reg. Temp. Ep. Roffen. Printed in R. R. p. 294. to 308.

Ordinatio penfionis Vicariæ de Darteforde, et Modificatio Dotationis Vicariæ de Darteforde, per Walterum Cant. Archiep'um. Dat. apud Lambeth, 4 kal. Aug. A. D. 1315. Reg. Joh. Fifher, fol. 140. a. (Printed in R. R. p. 302.)

DENNINGTON. See FRENDISBURY.
DOWN CHAPEL. See ORPINGTON.
EARITH.

No Account of the Endowment. Rectoria appropriat. Priori et Convent. Eccl. Chrifti, London. Act. Vifit. Archid. Roffen. 1504. fol. 9. b. — Compofitio facta inter Conventum

ventum et Parochianos de Lesnes de annua Solutione decem Solidorum ad Ornamenta et Libros Altaris Ecclesiæ. A. D. 1432. Reg. J. Langdon, fol. 99. b. Item Decemb. 20, 1400. MSS. Eccl. Cantuar. A. 11. fol. 44. b.

EAST GREENWICH. See GREENWICH.

ELTHAM, Vic.

The Rectory first appropriated to the Abbey of Keynsham, now belongs to Oriel College, Oxon. Act. Cur. Consist. Roffen. 1443. 1468. fol. 294. a.

Appropriat. Abbat. et Convent. de Keynsham. Act. Vis Archid. Roffen. fol. 7. b.—Advocatio concessa à Gulielmo Comite Glocestriæ Abbatiæ de Kayne, inter annos 1148. 1186. et Ecclef. Appropriat. Maii, 1242. Reg. Hamo de Hethe. f. 27. b.

The Tythes of Mottingham belong to the Church of Rochester, being antiently given to it by one Ausgotus of Chyſe Church; and though claimed by the Rector of Eltham, A. D. 1176, and by the Vicar afterwards, in 1234, yet, by the Judgement of Richard (Wetherſed) Abp. of Canterbury, as well as of Richard (de Wendover) Bp. of Rochester, both which Determinations are remaining among the Archives of the Church of Rochester, it was determined to belong to that Cathedral. Dr. Harris's Hiſtory of Kent, p. 117. Appropriatio Eccl. de Eltham, Abbat. de Keyneſham (ſans date) Aſſenſus Prioris Roffen. ſuper Appropriatione dict. Eccleſiæ. Dat. Roffen. kal. Junii, 1242. Chartæ Johannis Bath et Wellen. Ep'i ſuper Conceſſione dict. Eccl. Abbat. de Keyneſham. Dat.

ROCHESTER.

Dat. 6 Id. Dec. A. D. 1314. Conceſſio Decimarum Hamletti de Mottingham in Parochia de Eltham facta Monachis de Rocheſter. De Decimis iiſdem. (Printed in R. R. p. 334. et ſeq.)

EYNSFORD, Vic. (Peculiar Cant.) See AYNESFORD.

FARLY, Vic. See WEST FARLEY, Vic. Dotatio Vicariæ per Gilbert. Ep'um Roffen. Reg. Hamo de Hethe, f. 9. a. An Augmentation made to the Vicarage by Wm. Wells, Bp. of Rocheſter, and exhibited by the Vicar in a Suit with the Abbey of Leeds, Dec. 14, 1444, Act. Cur. Conſiſt. Roffen. 1444. 1468. fol. 17. b. 70. a. wherein is a particular Account of the Value and Endowment of this Vicarage. fol. 95. a.

FARNINGHAM, Vic. See EYNSFORD and FRENNYNGHAM.

Copy of a Decree of the Court of Exchequer in Favour of the Dea and Chapter of Canterbury, againſt Sir Anthony Roper, Knight, for a Penſion of 12l. per Annum, iſſuing out of the Manor of Charton, in the Pariſh of Farningham. Dat. 4. Nov. 1622. Chartæ Miſcellaneæ, vol. VI. N° 65. (MSS. Lambeth.)

FRECKENHAM (Dioceſ. Norwicen. Decan. FORDHAM in Comit. Suff.) Peculiar. Ep'i Roffen. Vic.

Vide primam Ordinationem dict. Vicariæ ab Ep'o Laurentio inter annos 1250 et 1274. Reg. Hamo de Hethe, fol. 230. a. Alia Ordinatio dictæ Vicariæ. Dat. 17 kal. Julii, A. D. 1347. Ibid. fol. 232. (Printed in R. R. p. 361.)

Anno 14 E. I. Epu's Roffenſis eſt Advocatus Eccl. de Frekenham ad quem pertinent. LX. Aer. hic redd.

per Ann. Ep'o 11d. faciend. tertiam partem unius fectæ Hundred. de Lacford. Regiftr. Abbat. Edmundi, fol. 111.

FRENDISBURY, Vic.
Conceffio Glebæ Vicar. per Thom. Ep'um Roffen. Reg. Spir. Roffen. E. fol. 13. b. Dat. Roffen. 7 Id. Sept. A. D. 1289. (Printed in R. R. p. 371.)
Conceffio Decimar. de Frendesbar, de Dennington et Suthflet, ad Prior. Roffen. per Joh'em Cant. Archiep. Dat. apud Halling in Craft. Purif. B. M. A. D. 1280. Reg. Cart. Vet. Conv. Eccl. X^{ti}. Cantuar. (In Bp. Moore's Library at Cambridge.)

FRENNYNGHAM (Peculiar Cant.) Vic.
Limites paroch. de Eynesford et Frennyngham Chartæ Antiquæ. E. 114. 128. (Penes Dec. et Capit. Cantuar.) Charta Stephani Archiep'i Cant.

Cant. de Ecclef. de Einsford et Frenningham, et de portione Vicarii de Frenningham, A. D. 1225, menfe Novembr. Chartæ Antiquæ. F. 52. Q. 173. et Regiftratur in Libro C. fol. 32. a. (Penes Dec. et Capit. Cantuar.)

Compofitio inter Priorem Eccl. Chrifti Cant. et Vicarium de Frennyngham Decanat. de Shorham, et Affignatio portionis ejufdem Vicar. Ratificat. per Joh'em Archiep. Cant. apud Lambeth. Die 20 menf. Maii, A. D. 1348. Regiftr. Liber dictus *Extra Kanc.* fol. 9, 10, 11. (Pen. Dec. et Capit. Cantuar.) Portiones affignate Vicar. Eccl. de Frennyngham per Dominos Priorem et Convent. Cant. (Chartæ Antiquæ. Q. 174. Ibid.)

Copia atteftata Compofitionis inter Priorem Eccl. Chrifti Cant. et Vicar.

de

de Frennyngham confirmate per Joh'em Archiep. Cant. 20 Maii, 1348. Chartæ Antiquæ. Q. 174. (Ibid.)

Dotatio Vicariæ de Frennyngham, per Joh'em Archiep. Cant. 20 Maii, 1348. Chartæ Antiquæ. Q. 175. quæ etiam patet in Libris magnis Reg. viz. B. f. xi. et C. f. 32. (Ibid.)

GILLINGHAM, cum LIDSING CAPEL. Vic. (Pec. Cant)

At Lidfing, is now a Chapel of Eafe to Gillingham, and hath been fo time out of mind. It is endowed with all Tithes, and here Divine Service is performed; but there are only feven houfes in this place. Dr. Harris's Hift. of Kent, p. 131.

GOUDHERST, Vic.

Reftitutio Decimarum Vicario de Goudherft per Robertum Cant. Archiepu'm

chiep'um Reg. Winchelfe, fol. 202.
a. 203. b. (MSS. Lambeth.)

GREENWICH, Vic.

Ordinatio Vic. 1218. Reg. Hamo de Hethe, fol. 28. Rect. appropriat. Priori et Convent. de Shene, Act. Vif. Archi'd. Roffen. fol. 7. b. Appropriat. Abbati et Convent. de Gant in Flandria inter annos 1188—1191. a Papa Clemente Reg. Hamo de Hethe, fol. 28. a.

Appropriationes Ecclefiarum de Levefham et Efte Greenwich (fans date) Regiftr. Joh. Fifher, fol. 81. a. Confirmatio Appropriationum predict. Ibid.—Compofitio inter Rectorem et Vicarium de Levefham. Dat. apud Lamehith, 10 die Maii, A. D. 1431. ibid. fol. 81 b.

HADLOW, Vic.

Ordinatio Vicariæ. Dat. apud Stone, 10 kal. Aug. A. D. 1287. Reg.
Hamo

Hamo de Hethe, fol. 12. b. (Printed in R. R. p. 381.)

Hallyng, Vic.
Ordinatio Vicariæ. Dat. 6 die Maii, A. D. 1538. Reg. Joh. Hilfey, fol. 196. a. (Printed in R. R. p. 400.)

Halstow, Rect.
Charta Laurentii Roffen. Ep'i concernens penfionem de Halgefto et B. M. in Hoo. Dat. Bromleghe in Craft. Afcenfionis Dominicæ. A. D. 1274. Sententia diffinitiva fuper Decimis Eccl. de Halgftow. Dat. apud Roffen. 21 Nov. A. D. 1476. E. Reg. Temp. Eccl. Roffen. (Printed in R. R. p. 404. et feq.)

Higham, Vic.
Ordinatio Vicariæ. Reg. Hamo de Hethe, f. 22. b. Capella S. Jacobi infra Eccl. Parochial. de Higham, Jan. 4. 1485. Lib. V. Teft. f. 68. b.

DIOCESE OF

Will of Wm. Roelf, who bequeathed the Church houfe, fol. 69. b.

HIGHAM, Rect. See LILCHURCH.
Appropriat. Prioriffe et Convent, Ibid. Act. Vif. Archid. Roffen. 1504. f. 11. b. et dein Magiftro Metcalf et Sociis S^{ti}. Joh'is Colleg. Cantab. A. D. 1523 vel 1524. fol. 11. a. 67. a.
Sententia lata per Commiffarium, Maii 19, 1523; et confirmata ab Epifcopo Martii 28 die, et ab Archidiacono Mart. 29. et a Convent. Roffen April 1. 15. 24. ib. 14. b. 15. a. Appropriat. Prioriffæ et Sanct. monialibus ibidem (fub nomine autem Lillecherche) inter annos 1166 et et 1183. Vicaria autem poftea ordinata fuit inter annos 1265 et 1298. Tempore Aufcticæ Prioriffæ. Reg. Hamo de Hethe, f. 22. b.

Hoo. See CLYVE, al. CLIFF, at Hoo.

Hoo All Saints. Vic.
Ordinatio Vicariæ 1327. Reg. Hamo de Hethe, fol. 76. Augmentatio Vicariæ. Reg. Hamo de Hethe, fol.
* 86. a.

Hoo, al. St. Warburgh, Vic.
Prima Ordinatio Vicariæ. Dat. apud Trottefclyve, 4 Non. April, A. D. 1327.
Secunda Ordinatio. Dat. Id. Mart. 1337. Reg. Hamo de Hethe, fol. 148. b. et Reg. Spir Roffen. F. fol. 16. a. (Printed in R. R. p. 423. et feq.)

Horton Kirby, Vic.
Appropriatio dict. Eccl. Magiftro et Confratribus Collegii de Cobham. 3 Ric. II. 1380. Tanner Notit. p. 227.
Ordinatio Vicariæ. Dat. apud Hallyng, 10 die April 1378. Reg. Joh. Fifher, fol. 79. b. Reg. Sudbury, fol.

DIOCESE OF

fol. 42. b. (MSS. Lambeth.) Printed in R. R. p. 431, et seq.

ISELHAM (Norwic. Dioc.) Peculiar. Ep'i Roffen. Vic.

A Determination of Benedict Bp. of Rochester, on a Dispute between the Rector and Vicar of Iselham, and the Convent of St. Jacutus *, about a Claim of Tithes. Dat. apud Frekenham, prid. id. Sept. A. D. 1219. Reg. Temp. Roffen. fol. Vac. ante fol. 1. (Printed in R. R. p. 437.) Concessio et Confirmatio Glebæ Vicario de Iselham, ab Ep'o Roffen. et Conventu. Dat Roffen. 4 Non. Junii, A. D. 1290. Reg. Spirit. Roffen. F. fol. 83. a. MSS. Eccl. Cantuar. A. 2. fol. 44. b. (Printed in R. R. p. 9.)

KEMSING cum SEALE, Vic.

Ordinatio Vicariæ. Dat. apud Bermondsey,

* A Benedictine Abbey, in the Diocese of Dole, in Britany.

mondsey, Oct. 13, 1402. Reg. T. Bottlesham, fol. 177.

Compositio super Ordinatione predict. Dat. in Monaster. de Bermondsey, 13 Dec. A. D. 1422. ibid. fol. 178. (Printed in R. R. p. 451. et seq.)

KYNGESDON, olim Vic. hodie Rect.

Augmentatio Vicariæ. Dat. apud Hallynge, 9 die Aug. A. D. 1436. (Printed in R. R. p. 454.) Postea hæc ecclesia de Kyngesdon convertitur cum Vicaria in Rectoriam per novam Compositionem temp. Rev. Patris J. Lowe, Reg. J. Lowe, fol.

LAMBERHURST, Vic.

See Particulars of the Endowment in the Register of J. Lowe, f. 211. b. Rect. Appropriat. Priori et Convent de Ledys, Act. Vis. Archid. Roffen. in 1504 fol. 6. a. Concess. a Rob. de Crepito Corde Canon. de

Ledes

Lædes et Appropriat. inter annos 1125 et 1138. Reg. Hamo de Hethe, f. 9. a. 10. a.

Dotatio Vicariæ. Dat. 7 Aug. A. D. 1447. Reg. W. de Bottelſham.

LEGHE, hodie, LIGTH, Vic.

Ordinatio Vicariæ. Dat. apud Roffen. 25 Feb. A. D. 1353. Reg. H. de Hethe, fol. 281. a. Alia Ordinatio, Dat. apud Tonebregge, 13 die Feb. A. D. 1393. Reg. W. de Bottleſham, fol. 46. b. (Printed in R. R. p. 464. et ſeq.)

LEWISHAM, Vic. See GREENWICH.

Chartæ Ordinationis Vicariæ. fact. annis 1218. 1289. Reg. Hamo de Hethe, fol. 28.

Appropriatio dict. Eccl. Priori et Convent. S^{ti}. Petri Gandevenſis *. (ſans date. E. Reg. Spirit. Ep. Roffen.) Confirmatio Appropriati-

* St. Peter at Ghent, a Benedictine Abbey in Auſtrian Flanders.

onum Ecclefiar. de Lewifham et Eftgrenewich per Ricardum Roffen. Ep'um. Dat. apud Trottefclive, A. D. 1239. ibid. Compofitio inter Rector. et Vicar. fuper Decimis. Dat. apud Lambeth, 10 Die Maii, A. D. 1431. (Printed in R. R. p. 470. et feq.)

LILCHURCH, Vic.

Ordinatio Vicariæ de Lilchurch, per Walterum Roffen. Ep'um. Hiis Teft. W. Archidiacone Roffenfi Magiftro R. de Lenham, &c. Ex Autograph. penes Magiftrum et Socios Coll. S. Joh'is Baptift Cantab. Printed in Monaft. Angliæ. vol. II. p. 885. and in R. R. p. 176. See Higham.

LULLYNGSTONE, Rect. et LULLYNG-STONE Capella.

Compofitio five Ordinatio fup?r Decimis inter Rectorem de Lullyngftone, et Capellanum de Lullyngftone. Dat. 8 die Oct. A. D. 1412.

Bibl.

Bibl. Cotton. Fauſtina C. V. f. 116. a. b. Unio Rectoriæ et Vicar. de Lullyngſtone. Dat. 23. April, A. D. 1712. Reg. Spirit. Roffen. (Printed in R. R. p. 477.)

EAST MALLING. (Peculiar. Cant.) Vic.

Ordinatio Vicariæ. Dat. apud Cherryng 5 kal. Mart. A. D. 1363. Reg. Iſlip. f. 202. a. b. (MSS. Lambeth) (Printed in R. R. p. 488.)

WEST MALLING, Vic.

Ordinatio Vicariæ. Dat. apud Hallynge 7. kal. Julii, A. D. 1339. Reg. Hamo de Hethe, f. 123. a. (Printed in R. R. p. 484.)

Sir Robert Brett, in the year 1620, gave 52l. (Taxes deducted) chargeable on an eſtate in Lincolnſhire, of 80l. per Ann. for the following uſes, viz. 10s. per Week for a Clergyman to read prayers and preach every

Satur-

Saturday in this parish throughout the Year, and 10s. to be equally distributed among 20 poor People of the Parish at the same time, who shall attend the Service. The Lecture is preached by five neighbouring clergymen, who are appointed by Trustees; but the Vicars of East and West Malling must always be of the Number of Preachers.

MEREWORTH, Rect.
Relaxatio super annua Pensione solvenda per Rectorem de Mereworth Monaster de Ledes. Dat. 20 die Nov. Anno 12 Hen. VII. A Terrier of all the Lands, Tithes, Profits, and Emoluments of the Parsonage of Mereworth, taken the 22d of July, 1634. From the Parish Register. (Printed in R. R. p. 497.)

MOTTINGHAM Tythes. See ELTHAM.
NETTLESTED, Rect.

United

United to Barming. See Barming.

Nockholt, olim Okolt. (Peculiar Cant.) Chapel to Orpinton and Cray.

The Boundaries of the Parish and Lordship of Okolt, anno 3 Regis Edwardi Quarti. Lib. dict. Extra Kant. fol. 18. a. (penes Dec. et Capit. Cantuar.)

North Cray, Rec.

Actum Juridicum super Unione Ecclesiarum et Parochiarum de Rokesley et North Cray. Dat. apud Croydon, Kal. April, A. D. 1557. Autog. penes, Dec. et Capit. Roffen. (Printed in R. R. p. 588. et seq.)

Northflete, (Peculiar Cant.) Vic.

Appropriatio Eccl. de Northflete, Reg. R. fol. 78. 79. 80. 81. (penes Dec. et Capit. Cantuar.) Portio Vicarii quadragina Marc. Ibidem. fol. 81. b.

Or-

ORPINGTON (Peculiar Cant.) Vic.

Charta Hugonis de Mortuomari Rectoris Eccl. de Orpunton, de Decimis Minoribus non petendis ex Manerio Prioris et Capit. Cant. de Orpentum provenientibus, falvo Jure Succefforum ejus, A. D. 1254. Chartæ Antiquæ C. 439. (penes Dec. et Capit. Cantuar.)

Rob. Say, D. D. provoft of Oriel College, Oxon. and Rector of Orpington, on granting a new leafe of the Parfonage of Orpington, abated 400l. in the fine, in confideration whereof the leffee was bound to pay annually an Augmentation of 26l. 13s. 4d. to the Vicar of Orpington cum St. Mary Cray, and of 13l. 6s. 8d. to the Curate of Down, a Chapel dependant on the faid Rectory.

This Leafe bears date 23 Auguſt, was confirmed by the Biſhop on the 30th, and by the Dean and Chapter on the 31ſt of the ſame month, A. D. 1687, and is entered in the Regiſter of the Dean and Chapter of Canterbury.

Copia Ordinationis Ricardi Cant. Archiep'i (A. D. 1173.) ſuper Vicar. de Orpington cum ſigillo (Archiv. Eccl. Cathedral. Cantuar. MS. A. 11. p. 38. b.) Proviſio Manſi et Aſſignatio parcelle terræ Vicario de Orpington per Will. (Courtney) Cant. Archiep'pum. Dat. apud Croydon, 9 die April. A. D. 1393. Confirmatio Prior. et Capit. Eccl. Chriſti Cantuar. predict. Aſſignationis. Dat. 20 die April. A. D. 1393. Reg. Morton Dene Bourchier et Courtney, fol. 189, a, b. (MSS. Lambeth.)

WEST

ROCHESTER.

West Peccham, Vic.

Ordinatio feu Compofitio Vicariæ. Dat. apud Bromleigh, 14 kal. Nov. A. D. 1387. Reg. Hamo de Hethe. f. 11. a. (Printed in R. R. p. 514.) Tithes belonging to it, as taxed 15 Edw. III. See MS. Eccl. Cantuar. A. 11. fol. 50. a.

Pembury, al. Pepingbury, Vic.

It appears by the Return to Bp. Bradford's Injunctions, by Mr. Richard Woodward the Vicar, 26 Sept. 1724, that there is an Augmentation to the Vicarage out of the Manor of Bayhall.

Appropriatio Eccl. de Pepinberi Abbat. et Convent. de Begham. Dat. apud Trottefclive, 9 kal. Dec. 1278. See Act. Vif. Archid. Roffen in 1504. f. 6. a. Decan. Oxon. S. Fridefwidæ proprietar. 1529. Fol. 80. a. See Reg. Hamo de Hethe, fol. 19. a.

Printed in R. R. p. 518. Granted to the College of Cardinal Wolfey, Oxon. anno 1528. (Strype's Eccl. Mem. Vol. I. p. 111. N˚ 29.)

PENSHURST (Peculiar Cant.) Rect.
Dimiſſio ad firmam pro Termino 99 annos per Rectorem Eccl. de Penſherſt unius parcelle terre Glebe ſue jacent. in quodam Crofts, vocat. Berecroft, jacent. ex appoſito porte Rectorie ibidem et continent unam Acram, unam Rodam, et 12 perticas, ad ſuperedificand. Reg. R. f. 111. b. (penes Dec. et Capit. Cantuar.)

The above Leaſe was granted by *John Acton, Rector of Penſhurſt, to Tho. Berkley, Clerk, Ric. Hammond, and Ric. Crundewell, of Penſhurſt, for 99 years, at the yearly Rent of Two Shillings, and upon Deaths or Alienations Twelve Pence to be paid for an Herriott. It is dated

ROCHESTER.

dated on St. Martin's Day, A. D. 1429, and was confirmed by the Abp. and also by the Dean and Chapter of Canterbury.

PLACKSTALL CHAPEL. See WROTHAM.

PLUMSTED, Vic.
Ordinatio Vicariæ. Dat. Cantuar. 12 kal. Aug. A. D. 1292. (Printed in X Scriptores Col. 2101.)

ROCHESTER, ST. MARGARET's, Vic.
Prima Ordinatio Vicariæ. Dat. apud Roffen. 21 die April, 1401. Reg. Joh. Fisher, fol. 83. a. b. Compositio dict. Vicariæ. Dat. in Fest. Purificationis B. M. A. D. 1488. Reg. Ric. Fitz James, fol. 37. a. Copia Augmentationis Vicariæ, MS. Eccl. Cathedral. Cantuar. A. 11. fol. 144. b. These and several other Instruments relating to this Parish, and that of

DIOCESE OF

St. Nicholas, at Rochester, are printed in R. R. from p. 559 to p. 588.

ROCHESTER ST. NICHOLAS, Vic. See ROCHESTER ST. MARGARET.

Fuit olim altare parochiale in Eccl. S. Andreæ una cum Eccl. S. Margaret, quæ appendit ex Orig. penes Dec. et Cap. Roffen.—Appropriat. cum Capella S. Margarettæ Monaſt. Roffen. inter annos 1147 et 1183. Reg. Hamo de Hethe, fol. 30. a. Reg. W. Wode, f. 1. a.—Bibliotheca. Cotton Domitian, A. X. 9. fol. 128. a. et fol. 98.

ROCHESTER CHURCHES.

In the Hiſtory and Antiquities of Rocheſter, printed at Rocheſter, 12°. 1772.—See an Account of the Church of St. Nicholas at Rocheſter, p. 201.—of St. Margaret's Church, p. 232.—of Chatham Church, p. 265, and of Strood Church, p. 241.

ROKES-

ROCHESTER.

ROKESLEY, Rect. See NORTH CRAY.

RYARSH, Vic.
Ordinatio Vicariæ. Dat. Roffen. in Craft. B. Andree Apoftoli, A. D. 1242. Reg. Hamo de Hethe, f. 22. a. et Bibl. Cotton Cleopatra. C, VII. f. 212. (Printed in R. R, p. 597.)

SHOREHAM, (Peculiar Cant.) Vic.
Ordinatio Vicariæ. Dat. apud Lambeth, 16 die Jan. A. D. 1380. Reg. Sudbury, f. 73. a. (MSS. Lambeth.)

SHOREHAM cum OTFORD (Peculiar Cant.) Vic.
Inftrument of erecting a Vicarage there, anno 23 Hen. VIII.—A ward concerning Tithes of Wood due to the Vicar, in a thin Parchment Book in the Library of the Dean and Chapter of Weftm'nfter, p. 34.
The Impropriation in the Dean and Chapter of Weftminfter. Lord Willoughby of Broke is Leffee; the

Curate has 20l. per Ann. as by Letter to the late Dr. Browne Willis, from Mr. Pugh, Curate thereof. Dat. Feb. 7, 17$\frac{12}{9}$.

SHORNE, Vic.

D'n's Will. Pepyr, Vicarius, legavit fuccefforibus fuis Vicariis Meffuagium fuum in quo inhabitavit, fic quod non vexent Executores pro reparatione Vicariæ, ex Teftamento fuo. Dat. Jan. 27, 1470. Lib. IV. f. 50. b. Archiv. Roffen.

Thomas Page, of Shorne, by Will, dated June 1, 1495, invefts in the Vicar and Truftees his Tenement, called Normans, lying and being in Upper Shorne, for a Dwelling houfe for the Vicar, as long as the World fhall endure. Lib. v. f. 273. b. (ibid.) Appropriat Prioratui Sti. Salvatoris de Bermundefeya, Reg. Temporal. Roffen. fol. 78. a.

Appro-

ROCHESTER. 201

Appropriatio Ecclefiar. de Cobham et Shornes Eccl. S. Salvatoris de Bermundefeya Reg. J. Fifher, fol. 97. a. Confirmatio Appropriationis Ecclefiar. predict. per Thomam Cant. Archiep'um, ibid. (Printed in R. R. p. 229, 230.)

SNODELAND, Rect.

Concordia fuper Decimis inter Rectores de Snodeland et de Waldeham. Dat. apud Trottefclyve, 24 die Sept. A. D. 1402. Reg. J. Botelefham, fol. 180. b. (Printed in R. R. p. 605.)

SOUTHFLETE. See FRENDISBURY.

STANSTED CHAPEL.

Chapel to Wrotham, according to Ecton.

Kilburn, p 255. fays, " This Parifh
" was formerly parcel of the
" Parifh of Wrotham; and the
" now Church here, a Chapel
" to that Parifh Church; but
" about

DIOCESE OF

" (about 13 years since) this
" Stansted was made a Parish by
" Parliament." See WROTHAM.

STOKE, Vic.

Ordinatio Vicariæ. Reg. Hamo de Hethe, f. 31. b. Taxatio Vicariæ (sans date) Reg. Fisher. (Printed in R. R. p. 622.)

Ordinatio Vicariæ per Walter. de Cantalupe, Wigorn. Ep'um. Dat. apud Blekeleigh, in Fest. Epiph. A. D. 1242. (Reg. Vet. Cart. Eccl. Christi Cant. in Bp. Moore's Library at Cambridge.)

STROODE. See ROCHESTER CHURCHES.

SUTTON at HONE, Vic.

Appropriatio Capellæ de Kingesdune in Paroch. de Sutton, per Benedictum Roffen. Ep'um, et Ordinatio Vicariæ (sans date) Bibl. Cotton Domitian A. X 9.—Appropriatio Eccl. de Suttone cum Capellis de Kingesdowne

ROCHESTER.

downe et Wilmingtone Prior. et Convent. Roffen. Dat. apud Lambethe, A. D. 1253. in Craft. S. Katharine Virginis. Autog. penes Dec. et Capit. Roffen. Ordinatio altera Vicar. de Kingefdune et Sutton. Dat. apud Hallinge 9 die Aug. A. D. 1436. Reg. Temp. Roffen. fol. 130. a. (Printed in R. R. p. 653, 654, 656.) This Vicarage is endowed with Hay, Wood, and other fmall Tithes, and with about 24 Acres of Glebe. It hath an old Penfion of 4 Nobles per ann. and of Wheat, Rye, Barley, and Peafe, out of the Parfonage; and fince the Reformation there is an Augmentation to it of 10l. per ann. Dr. Harris's Hift. of Kent, p. 306.

SUTTONE, Vic. et WILMINGTONE, Vic.

Compofitio inter G. Ep'um Roffen.

et

et Priorem et Convent. ejufdem Ecclefiæ de Advocationibus et Decimis diverfarum Ecclefiarum, in qua affignantur Portiones Vicar. de Suttone et Wilmingftone, Reg. G. fol. 286. b. (penes Dec. et Capit. Cantuar.) The Leffee of Sutton at Hone is to pay yearly to the Vicar 20 Bufhels of Wheat; alfo to the Vicar of Wilmington one Quarter of Wheat, one Quarter of Rye, one Quarter of Barley, and one Quarter of Peafe, with the Annual Penfion of 26 Shillings and 8 Pence in Money. Parliamentary Survey of the Manor and Rectory of Sutton at Hone, dated Jan. 9, 1649. (MSS. Lambeth.)

TERRIERS.

Thofe of the Archbifhop's Peculiars are now (1781) depofited in the Record Room over the Gateway of Lambeth Palace, and are under the

ROCHESTER.

the Cuſtody of the Archbiſhop's Receiver.

TESTON, al. TERSTON, Vic.
Appropriatio Rector de Teſton Priorat. et Convent. de Ledys Act. Viſ. Archid. Roffen. in 1504. fol. 4. b. Conceſſ. a Rob. de Crepito Corde Canon. de Ledes et Appropriat. inter annos 1125 et 1138. Reg. Hamo de Hethe, f. 9. a. 10. a.

TUDELY, Vic.
Ordinatio Vicariæ. Dat. in Eccl. Cathedral. Roffen. 17 die Sept. A. D. 1398. Reg. W. Botleſham. f. 120. a.

TUNBRIDGE, Vic.
Appropriatio Rectorie Prior. et Convent. Sti. Joh'is Jeruſalem Act. Viſ. Archid. Roffen. in 1504. fol. 5. b. Vide Appropriationem inter annos 1147. et 1183. Reg. Hamo de Hethe, f. 12. a.

WATRINGBURY, Vic.

Appropriatio Rectoriæ Priori et Convent. de Ledys Act. Vif. Archid. Roffen. in 1504. fol. 4. a.

Ecclefia conceffa Priori et Convent. de Ledes ab Hamone Filio Ricardi de Watringberry, inter annos 1104 et 1176. Reg. Hamo de Hethe, f. 9. b.

WESTERHAM, cum Capell. de EDENBRIDGE, Vic.

Ordinatio Vicariæ temp. Hamo Hethe Reg. H. de Hethe, fol. 37. a.

Appropriatio dict. Eccl. Prior. et Convent. Eccl. Chrifti Cant. et Taxatio Vicariæ. Dat. apud Hallynge, 25 die Jan. A. D. 1327. Reg. Priorat. Eccl. Chrifti Cantuar. (Printed in R. R. p. 679. et feq.

WEST FARLEY, Vic.

Appropriatio dict. Eccl. Monafter. de Ledis et Ordinatio Vicariæ (fans date),

date), Reg. Spir. Eccl. Roffen. (Printed in R. R. p. 353.)

WOLDEHAM, Rect. See SNODELAND.

Memorandum de Decimis quæ pertinent ad Abbatiffam de Mallinge in parochia de Woldham et inquificio facta per Thomam de Alkham et tenentes ibid. 26 E. III. Reg. Eccl. Roffen. (Printed in R. R. p. 694.)

WROTHAM, (Peculiar Cant.) Vic. See STANSTED Chapel.

Ordinatio Vicariæ (fans date), fed circa A. D. 1364. Reg. Iflip. f. 205. a. (MSS. Lambeth.)

Declaratio D'ni Tho. Arundell, Cant. Archiep'i, fuper portione Vicar. de Wrotham. Dat. apud Otteford. 7 die Jan. A. D. 1402. Reg. Arundell, pars 1ma. f. 357. b. (MSS. Lambeth.)

Licentia

Licentia habitantibus juxta Capellam de Plaxtoll infra limites parochiæ de Wrotham Divina Officia Audiendi et Sacramentum Euchariftæ recipiendi in dicta Capella. 8 Dec. 1711. This is extant in the Archbifhop of Canterbury's Entry Book. VI. 65. (It had been antiently ufed for Religious Offices.)

An Order and Directions fet down by Dr. King, &c. touching a Courfe to be obferved by the Affeffors to their Taxations of the Church, and the Walls of the Church-yard of Wrotham, in Kent, and to be applied generally upon Occafions of like Reparations to all Places in England whatfoever. (Godolphin's Abridgement of the Ecclefiaftical Laws. Appendix, p. 10. Quarto, 1687.)

WYL-

WYLMINGTON, Vic. See SUTTON, at HONE. See SUTTONE and WILMINGTONE.

Augmentatio Vicariæ. Dat. in Hospital. de Strode, 28 die Julii, A. D. 1436. E. Reg. Spirit. Ep'i Roffen. (Printed in R. R. p. 689.)

YALDING, Vic.

Ordinatio Vicariæ. 3 Kal. Mart. anno 22 H. de Hethe. (Printed in R. R. p. 145.)

In 1528, this Rectory was granted to Card. Wolfey's College at Oxford. Strype, Eccl. Mem. Vol. I. p. 11. Appendix. N° 29. Habuit olim Eccl. de Brenchelfey pro Capella fua.

INDEX OF CHURCHES

IN THE

Diocese of Canterbury.

Aldington, p. 1. 129		Bredgar,	p. 11
Aldintone,	1	Brokland,	ib.
Alkham,	2	Bromfield,	ib.
Appledore,	ib.	Brook,	12
Ash,	ib.	Cantuar.	ib.
Ashford,	3	—Sti. Dunstani,	13
Babchild,	ib.	—St. Gregory,	15
Beakisbourn,	4	—Stæ. Margaretæ,	16
Beauxfield,	6	—Sti. Martini,	ib.
Berfrestone,	7	—Stæ. Mariæ,	17
Bethersden,	ib.	—de Bredene,	18
Biddenden,	7. 130	—Sti. Johannis,	ib.
Bockland,	8	—Sti. Pauli,	ib.
Bocton,	ib.	—Sti. Petri,	19
Bonington,	9	Challock,	21
Boughton,	ib.	Charlton,	ib.
Boxle,	ib.	Chart,	ib.
Brabourne,	10	Chart Magna,	22
Bradsole,	11	Chartham,	23
		Chistelett,	24

Clyve,

INDEX.

Clyve, Stæ. Margarettæ,	p. 25	Goudherft,	p. 52
		Graveney,	ib.
Colrede,	ib.	Guffitona,	53
S. S. Cofmi et Damiani,	31	Hackington,	55
		Halftowe,	56
Cranebroke,	32	Hardres,	59
Deal Chapel,	34	Haftingley,	ib.
Debtling,	ib.	Hawkhurft,	60
Doddington, olim Dudintunia,	35	Hawking, al. Hakinge,	ib.
Dovor,	36	Hedcorn,	61
Eaftbregge,	ib.	Herbledowne, Sti. Nicholai,	ib.
Eaftchurch,	38		
Eaft Langdon,	ib.	Herne,	62
Eaft Sutton,	39	Hernhill,	63
Eaftry,	ib.	Hollingbourn,	ib.
Eaftry, et B. Mariæ Sandwici,	41	Hope, juxta Romney,	64
Egerton,	43	Hollingborne,	65
Elham,	44	Honeychild Manor,	66
Elmftede,	47		
Ewell,	ib.	Hothe,	ib.
Eythorn,	ib.	Hougham, olim Hugham,	67
Fairfield,	48		
Fawkenherft,	ib.	St. John Baptift, in Thanet,	68
Feverfham,	ib.		
Folkftone,	49	Iwade, al. Wade,	69
Godmarfham,	51	Kenarton, al. Kenardington,	ib.
Godwynefton,	52		
Goodneftone,	132	Kenyngton,	70

P 2   Kyn-

INDEX.

Kyngefnode,	p. 70	Nonyuton,	p. 86
Sti. Laurentii, in Thanet,	71	Norborne, Norborne, cum	87
Leeds, cum Bromfeild,	ib.	Shoulden, Ofpringe,	87 132
Lenham,	ib.	Oftenhanger, al.	
Leyfdown,	72	Eaftingher,	87
Lide,	73	Otringdenne,	88
Littleburne,	ib.	Overland Chapel,	ib.
Livingeburn,	74	Owre, al. Oare,	89
Loofe Chapel,	ib.	Patrikesbourn,	ib.
Lydden,	75	St. Peter, in the	
Lynfted,	ib.	Ifle of Thanet,	ib.
Lynton,	ib.	Petham,	90
Maidftone,	76	Pevington,	ib.
Marden,	77	Pluckley,	91
Menftre,	ib.	Poplefhale,	ib.
Midley,	79	Poftling,	ib.
Middleton,	ib.	Prefton, juxta	
Milton, juxta Sittingbourn,	80	Wingham, Reculver,	ib. 93
Monketon,	ib.	Rippele,	97
Nackington,	81	Kolvynden,	ib.
Newchurche,	82	Old Rumney,	98
Newenden,	ib.	Romenal, hodie	
Newington,	83	New Rumney,	ib.
Newfole Capella, Sti. Nicolai, et Omnium Sanctorum, in Thanet,	84 ib.	Saltwode, cum Hythe, Sandwich, St. Clement,	100 ib.

S and-

INDEX.

Sardwich, B. Mariæ,	p. 101	Thorneham,	p. 110
Sellyng,	ib.	Thrulegh, al. Throwley,	111
Sefalter, et Hernhill,	ib.	Tilmenston,	112
		Tonge,	113
Sheldwick,	102	Tunstall,	114
Sheperdswell, al. Sybertefwealde,	103	Uppechirche,	ib.
		Walderfhare,	115
Smallhithe,	104	Walmere,	ib.
Snargate,	105	Waltham, et Petham,	116
Snaves,	ib.		
Stalesfield,	ib.	Warehorne,	117
Stanford Chapel,	ib.	Westbere,	ib.
Stapleherst,	ib.	West Clive,	118
Stodmersh,	106	Westheth,	119
Stokebury,	ib.	Westwell,	ib.
Stone Chapel to Tenham,	ib.	Whitstaple,	121
		Winghorn,	122
Stone in Oxene,	107	Woodchurch,	ib.
Sturmouth,	108	Woodnesborne,	ib.
Sturreye,	109	Wotton,	125
Swinckfield,	ib.	Wycham,	ib.
Tanterden,	ib.	Wye,	126
Tenham,	110	Wyvelesbergh,	127
Thanington,	ib.		

INDEX OF CHURCHES

IN THE

DIOCESE OF ROCHESTER.

Aylesford,	p. 159	Darenth,	p. 172
Aynesford,	160	Darteford,	173
Barming, al. Bar-		Dennington,	174
minge,	161	Down Chapel,	ib.
Bexley,	ib.	Earith,	ib.
Birling,	163	East Greenwich,	175
Bradstede	ib.	Eltham,	ib.
Brenchley,	ib.	Eynsford,	177
Burham,	164	Farly,	ib.
Chalke,	165	Farningham,	ib.
Chatham,	ib.	Freckengham,	178
Cheslefeild,	ib.	Frendisbury,	179
Chevening,	166	Frennynham,	ib.
Chidingston,	ib.	Gillingham,	181
Clyve, al. Cliffe,		Goudherst,	ib.
at Hoo	167	Greenwich,	182
Cobham,	170	Hadlow,	ib.
Cowdham,	ib.	Hallyng,	183
Cray, St. Mary		Halstow,	ib.
Chapel,	171	Higham, Vic.	ib.
Cuxton, al. Cook-		Higham, Rect.	184
stone,	ib.	Hoo,	ib.
			Hoo

INDEX.

Hoo All Saints, p. 185
Hoo, al. St. Warburgh, ib.
Horton Kirby, ib.
Iſelham, 186
Kemſing cum Seale, ib.
Kyngeſdon, 187
Lamberhurſt, ib.
Leghe, 188
Lewiſham, ib.
Lilchurch, 189
Lullyngſtone, 189
Eaſt Malling, 190
Weſt Malling, ib.
Mereworth, 191
Mottingham, ib.
Nettleſted, ib.
Nockholt, 192
North Cray, ib.
Northflete, ib.
Orpington, 193
Weſt Peccham 195
Pembury, al. Pepingbury, ib.
Penſhurſt, 196
Plackſtall Chapel, 197
Plumſted, ib.
Rocheſter, St. Margaret's, ib.
Rocheſter, St. Nicholas, p. 198
RocheſterChurches, ib.
Rokeſley, 199
Ryarſh, ib.
Shoreham, ib.
Shoreham, cum Otford, ib.
Shorne, 200
Snodeland, 201
Southflete, ib.
Stanſted Chapel, ib.
Stoke, 202
Stroode, ib.
Sutton at Hone, ib.
Suttone et Wilmingtone, 203
Terriers, 204
Teſton, al. Terſton, 205
Tudely, ib.
Tunbridge, ib.
Watringbury, 206
Weſterham, cum Edenbridge, ib.
Weſt Farley, ib.
Woldeham, 207
Wrotham, ib.
Wylmington, 209
Yalding, ib.

FINIS.

www.ingramcontent.com/pod-product-compliance
Lightning Source LLC
Chambersburg PA
CBHW031827230426
43669CB00009B/1252